His Five Smooth Stones

His Five Smooth Stones

HERM WEISKOPF

Fleming H. Revell Company
Old Tappan, New Jersey

Permission to quote from the following songs is gratefully acknowledged:

From "A Bell Is No Bell," Copyright © 1959 by Richard Rodgers & Oscar Hammerstein. Williamson Music Co., owner of publication and allied rights for the Western Hemisphere and Japan. International Copyright Secured. All Rights Reserved. Used by permission.

From "Revolution" by John Lennon and Paul McCartney. © 1968 Northern Songs Limited. All rights for the U.S.A., Mexico and the Philippines controlled by Maclen Music, Inc. in care of ATV Music Corp. Used by permission. All rights reserved.

From "Which Way the Wind Blows," "Goin' Home," "With Jesus," "The Devil's Lost Again," "Love, Peace, Joy," and "I Don't Wanna Go Home," on the album *The Second Chapter of Acts With Footnotes,* Copyright © 1973 by the Latter Rain Music Company. Used by permission. All rights reserved.

From "YES MY GOD IS REAL" and "I'M GIVING MY LIFE TO CHRIST"
Lyrics and Music by Billy Preston
©1978 Irving Music, Inc. and WEP Music Corp. (BMI)
All Rights Reserved   International Copyright Secured

Library of Congress Cataloging in Publication Data
Weiskopf, Herm,
His five smooth stones.

    1. Bereavement—Religious aspects—Christianity.   2. Consolation.
3. Christian biography—New Jersey.   4. New Jersey—Biography.   5. Traffic
accidents—New Jersey.   Title.
BV4907.W43   1983   248.8′6   82-13304
ISBN 0-8007-1324-9

This book is dedicated to two women: my wife Jo-Ann, for her prayers, uplifting encouragement, love, friendship, and the belief that this book will be of help to people; and Mrs. Sue Kenkelen, who has made a ministry of helping people.

Contents

Introduction

The ring of a telephone in the wee hours of the morning, the pounding of the heart, immediate anxiety, the disoriented brain that seeks to assimilate what the ear hears, and the mouth that can only mumble unintelligible responses. Almost everyone has had this experience; pastors, I suppose, more than most. Sometimes there is a relief which comes with the inevitable "wrong number," but there are times when some sickening news sends the heart to heaven for immediate bolstering so that one can be for others, in a few moments, what he cannot be for himself at that moment.

In the early morning hours of Sunday, November 12, 1978, such a phone call awakened me from a dead sleep. It was sorrowful news. The enormity of the tragedy was not to be fully known for several hours, but the word was that at least one of our most dedicated Christian high school young people had been instantly killed in a grinding collision. (We later learned that five of our church's teenagers had been killed.) KILLED! That word "killed" still echoes in my memory, wrapped together with the sight of those five young people in their places of death amid crumpled steel and gouged macadam. It seemed so improbable. They had been doing something admirable only a few hours earlier—studying the Word together. How could they be dead? Is this God's reward for faithfulness? Questions came like a torrent, and most still remain unanswered. Especially for the parents: Barbara and Don Hayhurst, who lost Brian and Mark in the crash; Connie and Walt Van Beers, who lost Maria; Martha and Larry Carroll, who lost Tommy; and Mary Jane and Howard Borloz, who lost Eric.

Surely, none of us could have predicted at the time of the accident the full extent of the emotional turmoil that would be created, or the widespread and varied reactions that would be received. Or particularly, the lingering aftershocks that would ensue in the lives of the parents, the church, and many others who were touched in the days,

9

months, and now years following. Before the accident, we could have
postulated some very precise theological opinions on the nature of a
Christian's suffering, but on that November night the battle had to be
waged at close quarters without intellectualization. We were facing the
dark side of life, death in all its horror, and the events had begun
to overtake us. It became apparent that the only reasonable, faithful course was to yield frequently to the belief that, all evidence to
the contrary, God *was* in total control. Each time there came strength
for every little step, as glory was given to Jesus Christ all along the
way.

The parents of the teenagers were—for the most part—unprepared
for the gamut of emotions through which they would move. Any
casual reminder, every holiday, every anniversary seemed to bring
on tumultuous mood-swings: euphoria, strength, and victory played
against loneliness, weakness, and even for some, despair. We who
tried to minister provided some help, but we fumbled many times,
assumed too much, and responded too little. It became apparent that
pain (even long-term pain) and faith are not disharmonious in the
life of the Christian. We have all learned much of what it means to
bear one another's burdens, "and so fulfill the law of Christ." Burdens
and burden bearing are, in fact, conjoining aspects of Christian
living.

We were all unprepared for being in the middle of a "media event."
First, there was the attention from the New York television stations,
our north New Jersey community being only fifty minutes from midtown Manhattan. The story was carried by UPI and AP, and, of
course, there were front-page stories in the local papers. Later, there
came reactions from all over to the accounts of the deaths of five
"born-again" Christian teenagers, the faith of their parents, the tri-
umphant funeral services. Many were positive and encouraging notes
from people who were touched, who were stimulated to greater faith,
or who were simply fellow travelers who also knew what it was to lose
a child. But there were other notes and calls. A cult devotee wanted to
clarify, at length, where historic, biblical Christianity had supposedly
missed the boat on some esoteric point of doctrine. Even well meaning,
but hopelessly inaccurate evangelical Christians, hung-up on some
particular doctrinal issue, wanted to do battle with the parents, with
me, with anyone on matters ranging from the millennium to who in
the heavens is to be blamed for evil. I was impressed by how often

people can miss the whole point of Christianity as I observed the reactions of some of the misguided brethren.

The event and its reactions soon disappeared from view when played against the backdrop of a thousand "apparently greater tragedies" that were easily observed at the same time on this troubled old globe. The world moved on, but the effects remained in the lives of those for whom the tragedy is unforgettable.

One might surmise that a major personal disaster like this would inoculate against further tragedies, but such has not been the case. Most of the families have gone through other significant crises during the last several years. It is no easier to know the mind of the Lord now than in the first hours after the accident. Yet no one has lost faith, and for virtually everyone connected with the accident, faith in the risen Christ is firm and increasing. This is the record we hold to be so important today. There really is no other answer to life. I am reminded of Luther's great hymn, which says,

> And tho this world, with devils filled,
> Should threaten to undo us,
> We will not fear, for God hath willed
> His truth to triumph thru us.

The one fact that remains is that Christians also meet life head-on, suffering the same things others suffer, feeling the same things others feel, but yet there is a difference. Christians live on the basis of a higher Truth that remains in place despite outward appearances. They live by the word of the Apostle Paul which says, "The sufferings of this present time are not worthy to be compared with the glory that is to be revealed to us." The present witness of the Spirit of God to the heart of the Christian controls his reaction to circumstances by assuring him of what shall be. We are learning that God is to be trusted even though He does not give a running commentary on His reasons for every event that overtakes us. This is what has become exceedingly apparent. God must be trusted with life. Even hindsight is not 20/20. He is totally and completely sovereign over all events.

If we are looking for simple solutions and an easy antidote for our suffering, the answer is not to be found in this account. If we are willing to look beyond to the truth that God is in control, and that He does minister hope continually to the hopeless, then we will discover the only answer there is to suffering, just as the people whom you will read about in *His Five Smooth Stones* have discovered.

This is the record of those who categorically declare, "Let God be true and every man a liar." It is the record of those who affirm, even in their struggles, that whenever one's own perception of what is real conflicts with what God says is true, the wise Christian will trust God's Word. This is faith. It is far from being Pollyannish. This approach to life works and it is borne out in the lives of those about whom you will read.

Dr. R. Fred Beveridge, Pastor
Pascack Bible Church
Hillsdale, New Jersey

Can You Hear Them?

Can you hear them? Can you hear their shouts, their wall-to-wall laughter? Not yet, you say. Wait a few moments. Ah yes, here they come. How can we be so certain? It's that onrushing noise that sounds like a zillion chipmunks arguing while a herd of yaks gallops across a tin roof. That, so to speak, is their theme song. Actually, that din is the cacophony of their yattering voices and scurrying feet, and it precedes their arrival. There. *There they are*—hoards of teenagers rumbling, tumbling, stumbling out of school on Friday, the gateway to the much-cherished weekend. This is an occasion to be heralded accordingly, and so the shouts and laughs are a few decibels louder than at the end of any other school day. Friday. A special day. Young people's thoughts and even their footsteps are propelled by an extra measure of excitement at the start of each Friday-afternoon-through-Sunday emancipation. It is a part of Americana. Weekends have a pulse of their own—too weak to be heard if one does not listen for it, too loud to be missed if one hearkens. It is the youngsters who provide much of this beat. How easy it is to *not* hear their sounds, their vitality. Among their treasures are the echoes of their words and deeds that become their soundprints in time. Those echoes *can* be heard.

It was mid-afternoon on Friday, November 10, 1978. Light breezes tousled the few remaining leaves on the maples, oaks, birches, elms, poplars and their cousins in the upper corner of northeastern New Jersey. A few more leaves flitter-fluttered to the ground, there to blend their golds, bronzes, oranges, browns and reds with those that had already left home. Leaves. It was as if they had rehearsed all summer for this annual change-of-costume extravaganza, a gala performance for which they were now on stage in their most lavish attire.

How silent are the leaves. They are given voice only when crinkled underfoot, swept into heaps or stirred by the unseen maestro of this fall orchestration: the wind. Leaves. Children. How much alike in certain ways. Both buffeted at times by forces beyond their control. Both so fragile. Both adding so much to the drabness of the world that continually calls to them. Both with beauties so often taken for granted. Both must move on. The leaves go silently. The young people go with noisy vibrancy. Can you hear them?

A weekend of respite, fun and anticipation lay ahead for the youngsters in the rolling-hills countryside of Bergen County's Pascack Valley, a twenty-five-mile drive north and across the Hudson River from midtown Manhattan. Some would whoop it up in the area by bowling at Montvale Lanes or by strapping on skates at Fritz Dietl's ice rink in Westwood or at the Montvale Roller Rink. For others, there would be trips to the local movies to see *The Wild Geese* in Westwood, *Grease* in Ramsey or *Midnight Express* in Paramus. Some would attend the play, *Annie,* in Manhattan. Many would go to high school football games or to New York's Madison Square Garden to watch a Sunday night basketball game between the Knicks and Celtics, or a Sunday night hockey game involving New York's two teams—the Islanders and the Rangers.

Some would indulge in more radical quests for enjoyment by boozing, popping pills, or puffing on marijuana joints. More than a few, in their desperate attempt to get kicks out of a world that already was sorely disappointing them, would escape from reality by sniffing heroin or by using hypodermic needles to pop it straight into their veins. This book, though, is not about such frantic extremists. It is about five teenagers who were genuinely excited about their weekend agenda, one they *knew* would provide the fulfillment and laughs that all young people crave. Among other activities, the five had three events they all looked forward to attending. On Friday evening they would gather with other members of Salt and Light, their church youth group. Salt and Light meetings were held in downtown Westwood, roughly two miles from the Pascack Bible Church in Hillsdale that sponsored the organization. A Saturday night Bible study would reassemble the five and a handful of others. And on Sunday they would all see each other again at the Pascack Bible Church, where they would attend Sunday School and the regular church service conducted by Reverend R. Fred Beveridge. To many teens, that sort of schedule would seem worse than having to go to school. Eric Borloz, Tommy Carroll, Brian and Mark Hayhurst, and Maria Van Beers, however, were turned on by their calendar of events for several reasons, the most important being that the five were born-again Christians.

His Five Smooth Stones

"And he took his staff in his hand,
and chose five smooth stones out of the brook. . . ."
1 Samuel 17:40

1

Mark Hayhurst

Peanut Butter on Liverwurst

It was early evening on a day in 1967 when—*zap!*—all the lights in the Hayhurst house went out simultaneously. What was wrong? Hadn't they been paying their electric bill? Or had a storm knocked down a power line? Neither. Sudden power failures were nothing more than part of what had become normal everyday life in the Hayhurst household since Mark had arrived some four years earlier. Wherever Mark was, commotion, calamity—or darkness—was soon to follow.

Actually, it wasn't quite *that* bad. But it was bad enough. After Don Hayhurst had replaced fuses and brought the lights back on that night in '67, he and Barbara hunted around to find what strange thing had provoked the instantaneous blackout. They found the answer under a bed. That's where Mark went whenever he knew he had done something wrong. Not far away lay a charred ring of keys, one of which Mark had obviously inserted into a nearby electric outlet.

The same pattern held true almost every time the Hayhursts searched for the child who had perpetrated the latest misdeed: Corinne, David and Brian could usually be found quickly; Mark was the missing one. His favorite hiding places were under beds, under tables and under the dining room credenza. Other youngsters played games of hide and seek, but for Mark it was a more adventuresome variation: seek and hide. He did a lot of seeking in those days as he sought to figure out how things worked, how much a certain object would bend before snapping, how fire could leap forth from tiny sticks, why a coffee table crumbled at the mere touch of a saw. The more Mark sought, the more he was sought for in those hideaways of his.

"Mark had to check out *everything,*" Barbara Hayhurst explains. "Just because he got shocked by *one* light outlet didn't mean he would be by the *next*. Once, he became fascinated by the light switch outside our little downstairs bathroom. Mark couldn't figure out how the light would go on *inside* the bathroom when the switch was on the *out-*

17

side. So he got a tiny saw and cut the wallboard so he could get a closer look at things."

Inquisitiveness was a trait that Mark's parents could take a measure of delight in, for it seemed to indicate that their youngest son had a probing mind. Impulsiveness, though, was not so easily tolerated. Alas, Mark was at least as impulsive as he was inquisitive. While he was yet a toddler, his crib had to be moved into the center of his room, the better to keep his restless hands from yanking pictures off walls, from knocking items off the dresser, from reaching for shades, curtains, lamps.

How impulsive was Mark? Well, when he wanted to put up some pictures in the basement, he did precisely that. Thumbtacks would have been just right for hanging those pictures, but they were upstairs. Three-inch nails were right there in the basement, so that's what Mark used—even if most of their length did protrude through the other side of the wall and endangered anyone who walked by.

And then there was the coffee table. "Was" is the correct word here, for Mark's impulsive carpentry transformed the coffee table into immediate past-tense status when his experimental sawing left that piece of furniture with only three legs. "Idle hands are the devil's workshop," some people insist. That may often be correct. In Mark's case, his *busy* hands were like Satan's assembly line. He was probably no more than four years old when his mother, after a trip to the Westwood 5 and 10, noticed that Mark had brought home something she had not paid for. To put it more bluntly, Mark had stolen something.

"He took something little—a whistle or a small toy," Barbara Hayhurst says. "I dragged him all the way back downtown to the store [a half-mile walk] and told the lady there what Mark had done. She said to him, 'Do you really want it, honey? You can have it.' I said, 'Uh, uh. Oh, no.' He had to learn his lesson."

Mark's days as a thief were short-lived. His days of involvement with pyrotechnics, however, were more prolonged. Don and Barbara knew that Mark had for quite some time been fascinated by matches. Thus, when his mother caught him with matches at the age of eight or nine, Mark was given a crash course in flame and fortune. Into the kitchen went Mark and his mother. There she gave him two large jars of matches, a stone to strike them on and a pan in which to deposit the burned remains. And then the lesson began, Mark lighting match after match after match. There were lots of little flames; a few times Mark

Mark Hayhurst

was unfortunate enough to singe his fingers, although he refused to utter so much as a single, "Ouch." When this session was over, the kitchen reeked of sulfur. It was worth it, Barbara felt, for surely Mark had learned his lesson and would never tamper with matches again. She was, therefore, shocked when her husband told her a week later that he had seen Mark around the corner from their house playing with matches. That, though, was the last such episode.

Drip. Drip. Where was that water coming from when it wasn't raining outside? Drip. Drip. Drip. Why was water coming out of the kitchen ceiling? Drip. Drip. Drip. Schplatt! What was that pond doing on the kitchen floor? Dripdripdripdrip. Schplattschplatt. Anybody want to go for a swim over by the refrigerator?

More times than the Hayhursts like to think of, Mark let the upstairs bathtub overflow. The other children were guilty of that also, but none as often as Mark. Mark also frequently forgot that he was syphoning water out of the aquarium in his room above the living room. He was simply too busy to watch the tub until it was full or until he had sy-phoned enough water from his fish tank. No sooner did Mark start one of those operations than his mind would flit to something else, causing him to wander off to wolf down a snack, make a phone call, sneak a look at television, get into a conversation with someone in the house or browse through a magazine.

It was during an October 1977 missionary conference at the Pascack Bible Church that Brian Hayhurst was particularly impressed by a speaker from Teen Missions International. His interest was piqued enough to cause him to send for further information about the organi-zation, which trains hundreds of teens during the summer and then sends them to mission fields for several weeks. By the time the litera-ture arrived, Brian had dropped any notions about getting involved in such an endeavor. But Mark read the material, was turned on by it and decided he wanted to take part in a venture of that type. After sending for and receiving more information, Mark committed himself to spending most of the summer of '78 with Teen Missions. He wasn't certain which of TMI's ten mission fields he would be sent to, but he was positive that he wanted to know more about missionary work and that he wanted the spiritual growth he felt would accrue to him.

"He decided to go that summer for several reasons," Barbara points out. "Corinne was going to be married in June of 1979. And Mark knew that the summer after that he'd have to get a good-paying job so he could put away money for college."

Just as missionaries must do, Teen Missions workers must raise funds for their own support. Mark was advised that he would need slightly more than $1,000. This had to be raised by obtaining fifteen or so "sponsors"—people who would pledge four payments of fifteen dollars apiece. The bulk of these funds was needed for transportation to TMI's training camp in Florida and then to the mission field.

The excitement that Mark felt about such a project stayed with him during the early months of 1978. As time fled by, though, other feel-ings and realizations crept in. Mark began to weigh how difficult it would be to spend the summer away from his family, his church, his friends, the comforts of home, and the pleasant way of life he had grown up with. There were also questions: What am I getting myself into? Do I really want to put in a summer of hard work for no pay? What's it going to be like slaving away in some part of the world I don't know anything about? How safe are planes, anyway? By the time in late June when his parents drove him to Newark Airport for his flight to Florida, they knew Mark was more than a little scared of what lay ahead. A snapshot of him at the airport clearly reveals his apprehensiveness. Mark had a right to be concerned: He was only four months past his fifteenth birthday and he was embarking on a journey that would certainly be the most testing of his life.

Teen Missions International, Inc. blossomed in 1970 from Robert Bland's vision for getting teenagers more interested and involved with missionary work. With the aid of Mrs. Gayle Will and Jim Person, Bland turned his dream into a reality and in 1971 had fifty-seven youngsters at the first TMI boot camp. By the summer of '78, Teen Missions had undergone vast growth. TMI is headquartered on Merritt Island, which is near Cape Canaveral, and during 1978 fifteen hundred teenagers went through its program. The first phase is a two-week boot camp, which is conducted at a jungle-like 350-acre complex. Here the youngsters, both girls and boys, are prepared for their mission-field assignments. They are taught how to perform tasks they will be given on the mission field: how to lay cinderblocks, dig ditches, mix cement, and much more. They are readied physically by going through rigorous training that includes scaling walls and swinging on ropes to cross over bodies of water. Through it all, there is a continual emphasis that these teenagers must work together as teams and that they must learn to walk more closely with the Lord.

Wakeup came at 5:30 A.M. for Mark and the others at TMI. That was when the public address system filled the jungle camp with the resounding strains of *The William Tell Overture.* Each day, there was much time set aside for spiritual growth—meetings for everyone in a huge tent and times when each boy and girl went off alone for personal study and prayer.

When it was time for everyone to head for their mission field assignment, Mark's destination was Honduras in Central America.

The objective there for Mark's TMI team was to erect a hangar for the use of missionary pilots who would bring supplies to this new outpost being built in Honduras. There, under the broiling sun, Mark and his team went to work. They found out there was more to be built than a hangar. Extras they had to build were outhouses, one constructed by the girls for their use and one by the boys for their use. On the outside of the boys' there was a note that said: "Call Area Code 800 for Reservations."

The teenagers also had to help out with the cooking and cleaning at the compound where they lived. Days on which they were scheduled for such duties were regarded as a break because it gave them a day off from more laborious jobs elsewhere and because it gave them some free time to do their laundry and to write letters. In one of Mark's letters to his parents, he said he had taken a liking to rocking chairs made out of native mahogany that were being sold by the Hondurans for what he felt was an excellent price. Mark had enough money to buy one for himself, but not enough for a second one that he wanted to give to Corinne for a wedding present. So he asked his parents if they could hastily send him the funds to buy a second rocker—if they felt it would be a suitable gift for his sister. They sent the money. As in Florida, there was more than ample time for Bible study, prayer and sharing with one another.

Most of all, though, there were the long hours of working on the hangar. Mark turned out to be one of the strongest and most agile members of his crew and, as a result, spent considerable time up in the rafters of the hangar applying the final turns to the steel rods that had been only pretightened before being hoisted into place. His mechanical skill proved to be invaluable in several ways, especially when it came to repairing the temperamental gas engine pump that brought water to the compound from a nearby river. Mark, it seems, was the most reliable troubleshooter when it came to getting the pump to function properly again. In a way, that seemed like a rather novel twist: Mark, who so often got in trouble because he used to leave the water running and running at home, was applauded in Honduras for keeping the water flowing at the compound.

The most traumatic moment of Mark's stay in Honduras came as the result of—here it is again—running water. He was down by the river adding water to a barrel of lime which was to coat the cinder blocks that had been used in erecting the hanger. Mark apparently added water too quickly to the lime, causing it to explode. Much of the mixture shot into the air. Some of it, however, sprayed Mark in the eyes. His eyes felt like they had been scalded. Mark ran to the river, knelt down and scooped handfuls of water into his face. No matter how much he washed, his eyes still felt like burning coals. After receiving some medical attention, his eyes cleared up. Not, however, before he had time to contemplate the possibility that he might lose his sight.

"When he got home, he told us that right then and there when he thought he might be blind he decided that even that would be all right because he knew the Lord would take care of him," Don Hayhurst says.

To have come to so firm a conclusion apparently had a profound and lasting effect on Mark as a Christian. It was a definitive decision, one that signified a willingness to believe that he could *completely* entrust himself to God's keeping.

Mark's team worked so efficiently that the hangar was completed ahead of schedule. So the teens put in a foundation for a home that would house the yet-to-arrive missionaries. That done, they went to work fencing in the airstrip and the compound to keep the wild animals away. This was no small task. Many large trees had to be felled and cut to length. Holes had to be dug for the posts that were cut from the trees. And then five strands of barbed wire had to be attached to the posts. When the time came for the return trip to the States, three major jobs—the hangar, the foundation and the fencing—had been finished.

Before the youngsters headed for home, they all went through a debriefing period. This was done to prepare them for their departure, their return to families and to help combat depression that some go through after having spent a summer on what amounts to a spiritual "high." Ever-bubbly Mark Hayhurst never came close to anything even remotely resembling depression. If anything, it was Mark's family and friends back in New Jersey who had to do a little adjusting. The first thing they had to get used to was the new Mark—new physically, new spiritually.

"It was like we sent away a boy and got back a man," is the way Don Hayhurst summarizes it. "He had a dark tan and his blond hair was bleached by the sun. When he had left, you could see he was scared. When he came back, you could see he was self-confident and so in charge of himself."

What was most impressive was his remarkably changed approach to life. This was manifested in two ways. One was the obvious end to his compulsiveness. For the first time, Mark thought before he acted. All his friends noticed this turnabout, but no one appreciated it more than his much-relieved parents. He talked at length about a member of his team in Honduras who had walked on top of a revolving cement mixer and who had done other such things. It was obvious that as Mark had watched his crew member he had seen the folly of it all and recognized that he himself had indulged in many such actions without considering the possible consequences.

Even Mark's speech had changed. Before going to Honduras, he had been a notoriously fast talker and frequently got his words jumbled. When he came back, Mark spoke more slowly—and for a while with a trace of a Southern accent. There had to be a reason for that. There was: Most of the people in his work crew were Southerners.

In other ways, however, he was the same. As well coordinated as Mark was in some ways, he remained clumsy in others. As his father puts it, "He was still spilling milk until the day he left us." One reason for his being off balance and awkward was that he had gone through another spurt of growth, one that left him six feet tall and a gangly 135 pounds. Mark's twig-like frame required that he wear suspenders to hold up the trousers to the uniform he wore when he played his saxaphone at Westwood High School football games that fall.

Another thing about him that did not change was that he was the personification of the definition of the word "son" that was printed on a birthday card his parents had given him. Mark liked it so much that he tacked it to a wall in his room. It reads:

> **son** n. **1.** a male offspring who always makes life interesting but who seldom makes his bed; **2.** a happy creature often found in the vicinity of a refrigerator, and whose total capacity for food can only be estimated; **3.** a lovable person who constantly outgrows his clothes, but who never outgrows his wonderful ways.

One of Mark's not-so-wonderful ways (at least not according to most people's taste) was his penchant for a sandwich of his own concoction—peanut butter on liverwurst. That was still part of the *old* Mark. The *new* Mark was more special than ever.

"Mark came back from Honduras a totally different boy," Barbara Hayhurst points out. "The aim of his life was changed. His goal was that other people would grow spiritually and *really* know the Lord and what it was like to walk with Him. There was something very spiritual between Mark and Maria. They had sort of a pact that if they had a problem, they would call each other and talk about it."

"Instead of arguing the way they used to, David, Brian [Mark's older brothers] and Mark now found they could enjoy each other in ways they never had before," Don Hayhurst adds. "That changed a lot of things around the house."

Another observation comes from Bonnie Furman, an active member of the youth group who was three years ahead of Mark in school. Staring straight ahead at the kitchen wall of her house most of the time, as if the precise words she searched for might be found there, Bonnie spoke slowly and with fondness. She said:

"Mark was a fun person. A bit reckless at times. Thoughtful. Smily. Full of life. I was having some problems. Mark said, 'Come on, let's go biking.' His concern helped. Nothing he could have said would have made things easier for me. But his concern did help somehow. In the spring of that year [1978] I was walking home from my job downtown. It was getting dark. Mark came along on his bike. He saw me and walked me all the way home. He talked about his plans. He wanted to join the Wandering Wheels [a group of bicyclers from Taylor University in Indiana who go on long bike trips to spread the news of Christ Jesus]. He said he was going to ride his bike a lot to get in shape for that. Mark ran a lot, too. He was frustrated because he was so tall and uncoordinated, and there was a lot of joking about that in the youth group." On the track team at school, however, Mark was showing promise of being a winner.

Pastor Beveridge's relationship with Mark differed from that of other people. "He had the quality of being able to get into my good graces by needling me," Pastor Beveridge elaborates. "Mark would pick up on things I'd said and would tease me. I think some of that was so I would realize he had been listening to what I had said. He also kept needling me about all sorts of small things—for preaching too long, for fumbling over a word, even my age. It was all part of a young boy who wanted to be noticed by me and who wanted to be my friend. I liked that. I also very much appreciated the spiritual growth I saw in him after he came back from Honduras."

Mark Hayhurst, the young rapscallion who sent his entire house into darkness one night, spent much of his life thereafter lighting up people. So what if some of his jokes were as stale as last week's bread. It was his perpetual good humor that was most vital, for it turned gray and grumpy faces into lit-up ones. So what if he spilled milk or soda on himself, or dropped potato chips on the floor, or tripped over his own feet. When it came to laughing about his clumsiness, nobody guffawed more than Mark.

One of the most remarkable things about this youngster was the thoroughness and swiftness with which much of his life U-turned when he realized fully that the love of Jesus was the most beautiful and important thing in the world. He wanted so much for everyone to have the same happiness he had found in Christ Jesus, a joy that surpassed by many lengths that which came from mere humor. Everyone seeks substance, fulfillment, beauty and purpose in life. When Mark found them all through Jesus—zap!—it was like sticking a key in a light socket. Instead of all the lights going out, however, Mark found that *this* key in *this* light socket—this meshing of he and Jesus—turned the lights on brighter than he had ever seen them. What Mark experienced was something profoundly real and it gave him a million-watt glow.

2

Brian Hayhurst

A Perfect Shot—Right into the Lampshade

Brian Hayhurst was not usually impulsive, but one day when he was a young teenager he just couldn't restrain himself. So he yanked open the front door of his house on Second Avenue in Westwood and did what he felt he *had* to do: He yelled into the night air as loud as he could. Then Brian closed the door, thoroughly satisfied that he had treated himself to this convincing demonstration that his voice was changing and taking on a more masculine timbre. Brian got such a charge out of his shouting-into-the-night ritual that he indulged in it quite often, using the back door as well as the front.

Growing up had its rites and, Brian felt, its rights. He firmly believed that those rights included defending his point of view and standing up for what he wanted. Trouble was, when Brian stood at his tallest he was no more than 5 ft. 6 in. and 130 pounds. Brian was genuinely dismayed when, after asking when he would have the broad shoulders and deep chest of his older brother David, his mother told him, "You won't. There's no way. You two are just built differently." It hurt him too, that he would never be as tall as Mark, who was three years of age when he shot past Brian, who was seventeen months older.

"Being the smallest and being the middle brother, Brian always had to fight for his rights," David says. "Brian was an independent and *very* determined person," his father adds. "He didn't want anybody to get the better of him, even if that person was bigger than he was. The ones he usually fought with were his brothers and he didn't mind if he had to take six punches and give only one of his own. Brian simply felt he had to get his point across. It was hard for Brian to come to terms with being small. We pointed out to him that it really wasn't so bad and that there were some people who were not tall but who had lots of physical strength. Near the end, he was lifting weights and he was starting to develop nicely.

"When clothes were passed down, they went from David [the oldest son] to Mark to Brian," Don adds with a twinge. "I think it was when Brian was about twelve that he said, 'You know, I never get *anything* new. And Mark's so hard on clothes that by the time I get them they don't look so hot.' That's when I realized how much the kid had been hurting. So, even though it was hard to spend money on clothes that we knew couldn't be passed down to one of the other boys, we bought him some clothes of his own."

Although he didn't mind taking his lumps in scuffles, Brian learned it was less painful to fight his battles in another way: with words. Argumentation, as he found out when he presented his appeal for new clothing of his own, was often more effective than a punch on the chin.

"He had a jutting jaw and when you saw it jut out a little further than usual, you knew you had an argument coming," Don Hayhurst says.

Brian's family had a nickname for him: The Lawyer. His determination to defend himself at almost any cost was borne out when he was about seven years old. This came when the family went Christmas shopping at the mall in Nanuet, New York, just across the border from New Jersey.

Don Hayhurst reconstructs the event this way: "We let the kids do a little shopping of their own. I walked into a toy store and noticed there was a commotion at the cash register. I also saw that there was a line of people waiting patiently behind Brian, probably because they found it interesting to listen to what was going on. What was going on was that Brian thought he had been shortchanged and was telling the cashier that he had more money coming to him. She was trying to explain to him that the difference between the cost of the item and what Brian got back was the tax on the item. I walked over and was sure that Brian would want me to take over his case and defend him. But there was no indication that he wanted my help. After looking at me, he turned back to the cashier. By this time, he was crying because he was so frustrated. But all through his crying he went through his argument again until he was finished. Finally, the cashier and I satisfied Brian that he wasn't being cheated."

"We called him The Lawyer because he'd argue with you for three hours if he had to in order to get his point across," Barbara says. "Brian would hash things out from every angle. And if he thought you

Brian Hayhurst

were only listening to him and not *hearing* him, he'd go through it *all* again because he insisted that you had to understand what he was driving at."

Brian may have been argumentative and somewhat pugnacious, but he also had a tender side. An example of this came when he was approximately ten years old.

"I don't remember what he had done, but it was worthy of taking him to the basement where I had my desk and where I kept a razor strap," Don Hayhurst says. "We talked over whatever it was that he had done wrong and Brian was convinced that he needed to be disciplined. When he saw that our talk was coming to an end, he said, 'Dad, I know you gotta spank me, but when you're done could you pray with me so I'll be able to stop doing those things I know I shouldn't be doing but which I keep on doing?' "

Although he was well coordinated and agile, Brian was more interested in music and in tinkering with cars, electricity, and carpentry than he was in athletics. He had put a lot of effort into repairing a

Karmann-Ghia and was anxious to get it running. That was because David had promised that if the car could pass the state inspection, he would buy it from Brian for $100 plus the cost of parts and labor. Brian's farflung interests and activities, however, made it difficult for him to find time to proceed with the work.

His masterpiece was his attic room. Fancy it wasn't. Functional it was. While lying in bed, Brian could reach behind him to an orange crate on which he had installed a makeshift panel of switches that controlled lights, radio, a small television set, stereo, and speakers. Morning wakeup music was just a flick away from his pillow. When his alarm clock would announce that it was time to attack a new day, Brian would reach for the orange crate, trip the proper switch and on would come the record he had picked out the night before. Those switches also came in handy in another way, like when Brian heard his dad heading for the attic after spotting a crack of light under the attic door long after bedtime. When such emergencies arose, Brian did not; he merely reached for his switches.

"By the time I got up the stairs to the attic, the lights would be out and he'd be lying in bed playing possum," Don Hayhurst says, a wrinkle of laughter tugging at the corners of his mouth.

Curbside junkpiles were like mother lodes to Brian, who retrieved half a dozen or more stereo speakers from them. When he got back home with his latest find, he would restore to the wounded apparatus the voice it had lost. Three such salvaged speakers were in the garage behind the house. But Brian had not yet had time to rig them up properly so that they would blare forth the music from his attic stereo outfit.

One of the niftiest of Brian's attic antics had to do with a lampshade he fastened just below floor level at the top of the staircase leading to his room. The lampshade served as his laundry chute. Not wishing to subject himself to the incredible ordeal of having to lug his dirty clothes all the way downstairs, Brian did what many inventive teenagers would do; he found a simpler way. His method was to toss his clothes under a table he had installed around the railing along the side and back of the stairwell, aiming the soiled items for the strategically located lampshade. When his socks and shorts and shirts dropped off the lip of the floor and into the lampshade, they would be funneled so they would drop perfectly in the corner at the bottom of the stairs. That way, his mom could gather them up without having to go up a flight of stairs to fetch them.

Still tacked to the slanting attic walls are evidences of some of Brian's industriousness: a calendar of youth group activities and a sheet of paper on which he kept tabs on the monies from his paper route.

Ah yes, the newspaper route. David was the first of the Hayhursts to deliver the local paper, *The Record,* which is published in nearby Hackensack. When the route became too extensive for David to handle, he split it with Brian. And when David went off to college, Mark took over his half. Both Brian and Mark earned almost $2,000 a year from this endeavor. Brian was anxious to branch out into other areas of work, so in June 1978 he turned his newspaper route over to Tommy Carroll, who lived next door. Among Brian's labors that summer were lawn mowing, roofing, repairing a swimming pool, babysitting, landscaping, and rebuilding and painting a neighbor's porch. Even when he finished his work, Brian did not stop working. He put in many hours to help spruce up the backyard for the reception that would follow his sister's wedding in June of the next year. To that end, he worked with his father and David at putting down sod, building a brick patio and finishing a six-foot-high stockade fence in the backyard by putting up the fencing along the entire left side.

Late in August, Brian took a break—he bicycled 380 miles to Webster, New York. This was a joint venture on which he and Bill Carroll (Tommy's brother) embarked, setting off at 6 A.M. on Monday, camping out at night and arriving at 6 P.M. on Friday at the home of Bill's sister, Mrs. Leslie Knapp. Tommy Carroll and his folks drove to Webster on Friday and arrived there a few hours after the weary bikers.

"They were numb," Larry Carroll remembers. "When it was time to head back to New Jersey, we put the bikes in our big van. Brian and Bill were only too happy to ride back with us."

Shortly thereafter, Brian undertook another form of locomotion that he had been hankering to get a taste of: driving a car. "He was the only one of the kids who was not uptight when I took them out for lessons," says his dad. "He knew what he was doing and he did it well. Brian had the same good coordination that he had in many other areas and he was always alert. I took him out to drive on Route 17 during the rush hour and I got him out on the Route 4 interchange, and he was like a pro. He was as calm as could be. It was Halloween day that he got his license."

Brian also displayed a growing interest in something else that year: girls. "Maria was working at a store in Westwood that summer and

Brian often stopped to visit her," Barbara Hayhurst says with a grin. "One day I asked him, 'Are you interested in Maria?' He said,'I can't make up my mind.' I looked at him kind of funny and said, 'I guess that's why you rode your bicycle downtown *in the pouring rain* to bring something to Maria that she really didn't need.' It was so typical of kids their age. They weren't all that sophisticated in their ways, but they were a pleasure to watch."

When Brian began dating, it was with another girl—Laurie Cole. "I guess you'd say we were dating," Laurie says. "Never alone. It was just *understood* that we were dating."

Pastor Beveridge had recollections of Brian driving around the church parking lot. "Brian caused a stir among some people because he was driving his dad's van around the church parking lot," the pastor says. "They were concerned that he was practicing in the place where lots of people were walking around. We had to deal with the situation and clamp down on him."

Compared to the thoroughly outgoing Mark, Brian was rather quiet. The more he became involved with the church youth group, though, the more he seemed to open up and try to reach out to other people. This was part of a growing and sincere concern he was developing for others. There were several proofs that this was so, among them a letter written two days after the accident to the Hayhursts by Ellen Baldauf:

> I wanted to let you know what Brian and Mark meant to me. When I first started going to the youth group, I felt very alone and out of place. The group had already been established and there I was coming in all by myself. It seemed everyone had friends from school who went there also. Brian was one of the people who came to me and made me feel like they were all my friends, and I was far from alone. He made sure that I and everyone else was involved in everything we did. He was like a light that was always burning brightly. I never told him how much he meant to me or how much I loved him, but I'm sure he knows.
>
> It wasn't until Mark came back from Honduras that I met him. Just like Brian, he again kept everyone involved and helped you out whenever you needed it. He seemed to always know the right things to say. If you were sad or upset, he could always get you smiling and laughing.

It was during the summer of '78 that a precious relationship developed between Brian and his mother. That was because, in addition to having eyes on girls his age, he had his eyes on another girl: his mom.

"Mark was in Honduras, and Corinne had clammed up and wasn't confiding in me the way she used to," Barbara Hayhurst says. "I knew it was natural and right for her to shift the sharing of confidences to her fiance, Ben, but I still missed it so very much. Brian could tell that I was hurting. He understood and he talked with me a lot. Brian was always good that way. David wasn't much of a talker. Mark was too young. But Brian *knew* when I was upset, and he reached out."

That was also the summer the three brothers experienced a new closeness. "Starting in August of that year, Brian and I became close friends for the first time," David recalls. "We ran the youth group for awhile that summer. I had never had as much conflict with Mark as I did with Brian. When he came back from Honduras, it was the three of us. By the end of the summer, where one of us was, the other two would be there, too."

There were other indicators during the summer and fall that Brian was maturing. As leader of the Slave Day money-raising project, he kept precise records and, putting his determination to use, made call after call after call to coordinate who was going to be available to do what job and when, and how they would get there.

Music had always been vital to Brian, who played the piano, was learning how to play David's drum, and had taught himself how to play the guitar. Aside from that, there was his stereo system and the records that he seemed to be forever listening to. Before Mark went to Honduras, he had been somewhat bothered by the rock and roll music that Brian favored. When Mark returned home, his feeling about the matter was more intense, so much so that he talked at length to his brother about the music. Mark urged his brother to get more into Christian music and to cut down his emphasis on other songs.

"We hadn't been happy with the music Brian was listening to," Barbara Hayhurst says. "Brian *knew* that Mark used to enjoy the same type loud songs, so when his brother talked to him about it from a Christian standpoint, he got the message."

"By the time of the accident, Brian was listening to strictly Christian music," Don Hayhurst adds. Shortly after the crash, Don went up to Brian's room. He noticed that the sneakers were lined up side by side with the laces tucked inside. In the past, Don would have been lucky if he could have found Brian's sneakers within five feet of each other. Don then saw that there was a record on the stereo turntable. Music had, as always, come from Brian's room on the morning of November 11th, and now Don was curious to find out what the last songs were that his son had played while in the attic. The album on the turntable was by a well-known Christian group, The 2nd Chapter of Acts. There were six songs on the side of the last record Brian had played: "Which Way the Wind Blows," "Goin' Home," "With Jesus," "The Devil's Lost Again," "Love, Peace, Joy," and "I Don't Wanna Go Home." Don tentatively fingered switches and dials so he could hear the record. At long last, he struck the correct combination. As the music came out of the speakers placed around the attic, he listened to the words and wept. Then he listened again and again, and he jotted down words from the songs on a piece of notebook paper:

You don't know which way the wind blows,
So how can you plan tomorrow?
Jesus knows which way the wind blows
So give Him your tomorrows.

Goin' home inside. There's an ache in my heart. . . .
Take my hand and lead me home, oh Lord. . . .
Help me wait on you, Lord, 'til the day you come.

Mile after mile I am walking and holding to the One who cares.
With Jesus I'm stayin'. With Jesus I'm goin'. . . .
Jesus is teachin' me love each day.

Look at me now. . . . The devil's lost again. . . .
The devil is a liar.

Love . . . Peace . . . Joy . . . Stop, think it over,
You can have these if you're born again. . . .
You'll have love in your heart. . . .
Don't you try to hide any longer.
'Cause you need love.

I don't wanna go home without sharin' the Word.
How He came to wash us with His blood precious
And I start crying.
Don't you wanna be free?
Things that hassle your soul, Keep your life from livin'
And your give from givin'. Are you dying?
Now you can do it from the start again
And change those things that you'd rather hadn't been.
Stop your lying!

Jesus offers the way
You can be born again.
All your past forgiven
And new life for livin'.
He's worth trying.
Now you can do it from your heart, my friend,
And change those things you'd rather hadn't been.
Stop denying!
Are you dying?
Stop your lying!

3

Maria Van Beers

Football Player, Puddle Jumper, and Missionary

She was champagne with curly, shoulder-length auburn hair, brown eyes and a face so chock full of smiles that it seemed even her freckles gushed with happiness. That smile—even with the clutter of braces on her teeth—was warm and irrepressible and as vivid as the brightest paints her father sold in his stores. And when that smile was accompanied by her giggles and laughs, why it was enough to have made Mona Lisa break out in a grin. Maria Van Beers was one of those rare people who got such a kick out of living that those around her got a kick out of her. That she brightened up lives was fitting, for Maria let life brighten her. She did not merely pass through life; she tested it and tasted it, flavored it and savored it. Most of all, Maria not only took from life, she added to it.

"Maria gave the gift of strength and support to us and to everyone she came in contact with," is how her father puts it. "She had the ability to see something good even in bad situations." That Maria was able to provide strength and turn a seemingly down-beat situation into an upbeat one can be seen in this piece of writing, which is part of a diary-type journal she kept for her advanced-composition course during her sophomore year at Northern Highlands Regional High School.

Girls and Football? Ha! Ha!

This year, a large number of the gym classes switched to co-ed, meaning the girls would be playing many sports they had not played before, such as football. My gym class had been playing football for the past week and it has become quite obvious to us girls that the game is being played by the boys alone. We girls are being told to block the players of the other team. Now let's be serious. What girl in her right mind is going to stand in front of a guy twice her weight and size and attempt to block him? Well, not us. So we complained. I personally told the quarterback on my team that I wanted a chance to receive a pass and then to give my other teammates (girls) a chance to get into a play. So he agreed, much to my surprise, and told me the play. I was to run down the left side and then cut in to the center to receive his pass. And so I did. I caught the football and was filled with so much excitement I screamed and threw the football into the air. The coach had been watching and was rather surprised by my reaction. But anyway, I'll tell you the new arrangement of our football team. My friend Judy is our new quarterback and I'm a regular player, much to the surprise of the guys on our team (who, by the way, are now blocking). Our team has played five games and we are undefeated. Now if other teams would look upon our example, more girls would be able to prove to guys as well as themselves that they too can play football.

During her first year in high school, she was editor-in-chief of the freshman literary magazine, *Timeless Thoughts*. Mrs. Rona Meyers, advisor for that publication and English teacher at the school, wrote a memorial to Maria in the school paper, *The Highland Fling*. While expressing her frustration with trying to find meaning in Maria's death, Mrs. Meyers wrote: "If only she had not been so vibrant, so interested in others, so curious. . . . she ardently worked to make last year's freshman magazine memorable. In addition to expending seemingly inexhaustible energy in preparing the publication, she contributed many poems and drawings." *Timeless Thoughts* included this item by Maria:

Time
Time is what you spend alone
in beautiful thoughts and dreams.
Time is not hours, minutes, or seconds
although that is what it seems.
Time is never ceasing. It's here
and always will be.
Time is beginning, not ending,
forever eternity.
Time can be peaceful and
happy when all around you is free.
Time is being born and dying
and a life that is yours
free to live.
Time is not what you take
from the world but the everlasting love that
you give.

Maria Van Beers

Whatever Maria did, she did with ardor. Except for two things: housework and cooking. "She would finagle all kinds of ways to get out of housework," Connie Van Beers says with a slight shake of her head. Ah, finagling, *that* was one of those many things Maria did with ardor. And that's why she was such a successful finagler. One example was the campaign she waged to strengthen her relationship with Brian Hayhurst. Maria knew she couldn't come right out and invite Brian to her house. So her first salvo in this battle was to urge her parents to get to know the Hayhurst family better. Try as she might, however, Maria couldn't convince her folks to have the Hayhursts over for a meal or for an evening's conversation. Just because the Van Beerses were too busy to promptly take up the suggestion was hardly a deterrent to Maria. If her parents weren't going to invite the Hayhursts over, then Maria would have to get things in motion herself. This she did by inviting *all three* Hayhurst boys to her house for dinner a few weeks before the accident. She also invited Beth Robertson, her best friend.

As much as she didn't want to, Maria knew she had to help her mother prepare the meal. While she puttered around the kitchen, though, Maria couldn't help noticing that Beth, Mark, Brian, and David were on the front lawn playing Frisbee. This wasn't at all the way she had planned things. *Something* had to be done. It was. Maria tried to cajole and con her younger sister Donna into taking her place in the kitchen. Donna was reluctant. After all, it was *Maria* who had invited her friends for dinner. Never one to give in easily, Maria did some further coaxing. The next time Connie Van Beers turned around in the kitchen there was Donna, taking care of the noodles.

Maria's power of persuasion would have been an asset had she achieved her career goal of becoming a lawyer. "She could also be super demanding, so much so that there were times I felt like tearing my hair out," admits Walt Van Beers, who refrained from such urges and still retains a bushy head of black hair.

There was another side to Maria's powerful personality that cut more deeply than she realized for a long time. Connie elaborates on it: "This is not easy for me to say, but I have to. Maria was *very* close to Walt. She was never as close to me as Donna is today. Maria was a very, very smart girl, and I have to tell you that at times I felt inferior. I was born in Holland and my English is not always too good. Maria would correct my English. Sometimes I would be sensitive about it and would feel insulted. She kind of overpowered me. I felt that she was above me. Maria and I had a tough year between the time she was fourteen and fifteen. Then I shared with her some personal experiences because Maria thought that I was very strict. After Maria and I had one of our disagreements, the Lord kept saying to me over and over to tell her what was on my mind. So I told Maria of my experiences and what had happened to me and why I was so protective of the girls. From that day on, she turned right around and her last year here on earth was so beautiful. We got along so well and the inferiority that I felt just went away. I feel the Lord gave me the gift of having a good relationship with her that last year. If she had died in the time when we did not hit it off that well, I would have blamed myself for being a bad mother."

That Maria considered Connie to be anything but "a bad mother" is evident from this entry in her journal:

My Mother
My mother's a special person to me.
Whenever I need her, there she will be.

When I'm in trouble or just need a friend,
She'll always love me right till the end.
As I get into my teens, and my freedom grows,
More and more her love for me shows.
Soon I'll be out with new problems to face,
But no one will *ever* take my mother's place.

"My last memory of Maria—the last time I saw her—was the night before the accident," Walt Van Beers says. "Before she left the house to go to the youth group meeting, I gave her a big hug. I'll always be glad that I did."

"In some ways, she was not terribly affectionate toward me," Connie points out. "There were times that I made her get out of bed to give kisses to us before she went to sleep. When I saw those signs that said, 'Have You Hugged Your Child Today?' I went to give her a hug, but she didn't like me doing that."

Maria might not have been much for smooches and hugs, but there was no doubt that she exuded warmth, tenderness, and compassion in large doses. Sharing her Christian faith was something else she frequently did, both with her peers and with adults. One of those grown-ups was Tom Cussimanio.

"On December 7, 1977, I had a chainsaw accident," Cussimanio begins. "While I was in the hospital, I got a note from Maria in which she included a couple verses of Scripture that she felt would encourage me. I thought it was so neat to get such a mature note from a young person. I've marked in my Bible the verses she sent to me. They're from 1 Peter 4:12–13: 'Beloved, think it not strange concerning the fiery trial which is to test you, as though some strange thing happened unto you, but rejoice, inasmuch as ye are partakers of Christ's sufferings, that, when his glory shall be revealed, ye may be glad also with exceeding joy' (New Scofield Reference Edition).

"Shortly before the accident, we had a group of kids here at the house. I was lying on the couch here and when the kids came in the front door they couldn't see me. [The foyer in the Cussimanio house is one level below the main floor.] I stuck my hand up to kind of say 'Hello' to the kids as they came in. They didn't see that. When I heard Maria's voice, I said, 'Is that Maria?' She saw my hand and said, 'Coos?'—she had recently learned that was an old nickname of mine. Then she came up the stairs and gave my hand a squeeze. We had a special kind of relationship and it was just like her to go out of her way to express her feelings like that."

Vivacious Maria. She could find pleasure in such a variety of things. Of her cat she wrote, "Squirt is the most beautiful and well-behaved cat I know. (She's even potty trained.)" When she wrote about Michael Doctor, for whom she was often a babysitter, Maria penned these lines: "I love to play with him and make him smile and watch his big, beautiful blue eyes light up. He even talks to me. He gurgles and makes all those adorable little sounds. He's a little pudgy thing. I call him my butterball." When Maria played her flute in the high school concert band it was with her typical enthusiasm. This zest for life can be seen in these two items in her journal:

> I'm in gym right now. I have a pretty bad cold, so instead of taking gym I'm gonna stay in the nurse's office. My mother didn't want me to be running around outside 'cause my cold could get worse and probably go to my throat. This is really boring. I think I'd rather be taking gym. Who cares if I get a sore throat?

Puddle Jumping
> On your way home from school, there it sits big, mushy and brown.
> So tempted to jump right in the middle.
> With mud splashed all around.
> Mom won't mind, you say to yourself.
> What possible harm can be done?
> After all, everyone knows that Puddle Jumping is fun.

For Maria, the whole world seemed to be a succession of puddles she could merrily splatter through. Joining her hand in hand and side by side through this puddle splashing—symbolic as well as real—were her friends. One of her closest companions was Laurie Cole, who helped with the preparations for a youth group Halloween party two weeks before the accident. ("We gave Maria a choice of having either a Halloween party or a birthday party," Connie Van Beers recalls.)

Laurie also has fond recollections of that event. "Maria and I made a tape of a ghost story and we played it at the party. Her mother was there when we made it and we all laughed so hard that the tape wasn't as scarey as we had hoped because everyone could hear us laughing. It was a dress-up party, and Brian and I went as the king and queen of hearts. Craig Cussimanio and Maria were a fifties' couple.

"Maria was such an unusual person. I don't think I *ever* saw her mad or sad. She wanted everyone to go to the youth group meetings and have a good time. Maria was the one who got me to join."

One of the ways Maria's strong will paid off was when it came to getting other youngsters to give the youth group a try. That was no easy task; teenagers usually have plenty to do and if they're not affiliated with the church it's often hard to convince them that good times could be had at youth group meetings. Persistence, Maria may have learned from her own case, was invaluable when it came to this sort of "recruiting." She had turned down numerous invitations from Bonnie Furman before she gave in and started attending the meetings. Soon, she was hooked. Then, as people often do when they come across something that really turns them on, Maria told others what she had found.

"She was a missionary," is the way Walt Van Beers sums up this trait of his daughter.

"Maria always yelled and pushed to get people to go to the youth meetings," Beth Robertson adds. "She recruited me. Others would say to her, 'Let's go to a party. Let's meet some guys. Let's get drunk.' Maria didn't give up on them. She kept inviting them."

"She was yearning for the day she could be baptized," Pastor Beveridge says. "I remember talking with her in the narthex of the church the week before the accident and making all kinds of plans for what the kids wanted to do in that service to make it special and significant."

"There were times when I'd drive Maria home and we'd sit in the car while we were in her driveway, and we would talk for an hour and a half," Craig Cussimanio remembers. "We had both recently gone through the born-again experience and we had a lot we wanted to share with each other."

Maria and her truest friend—Beth Robertson—had begun the groundwork for teaching a Sunday School class about friendship and its meanings. Friendships were extremely important to Maria, as can be seen from this poem:

Friends
Friends are special people who love and care.
Always there at your happiest moment and when
   you're feeling blue.
There with a helping hand when you're in need of one.
And a person who will listen, too.
But the greatest thing about a friend is,
You know they'll always be true.

Among the happiest memories the Van Beerses have are those of travels they often went on with the whole family. "We used to camp out and sleep in a tent," Connie said with a bit of a shudder. "After four years of that I said, 'I've had it with tents.' Then we bought a nineteen-foot trailer and used that for five summers."

"One of the trips we took was to Virginia," Walt chimes in. "We were sitting outside the trailer with another couple. We thought all the kids were asleep, but then we heard the girls giggling. They were laughing about a frog who was sitting on a rock near a lamp. He was sitting there and whenever a bug would fly by he would flick out his long, long tongue and gobble it up. Pretty soon, all of us were laughing while we watched that silly frog pick bugs right out of midair.

"The last trip we took with Maria was to Kent, Connecticut. That was in the summer of '78. I was trying to learn how to sail a sailboat and one day I took Connie out on the lake. Well, the wind took us all over—into the lily pads, into marshy water. I tipped the boat over, I got stuck in the mud. Then I took Connie back to the shore. Maria said, 'I'll go with you.' I told her, 'OK, but I'm running the sailboat.' I sure did. I ran it into the lily pads and we drifted all over the place. Finally, I got the boat out into clear water, but I couldn't control it. 'Let me take it, Dad,' Maria said. 'Really, I know what to do.' She had done a little sailing once so I said, 'OK, Maria, you try it.' She took over and that sailboat went just where she wanted it to go. She knew how to catch the wind in the sails and she took us all over the lake and then back to land. It was so beautiful."

Maria at times did not sail through life with the same ease as the sailboat did that day. She had her share of "bummers," although she had a remarkable buoyancy. Accepting Jesus Christ as her personal Savior had an enormous impact on her. She learned that she didn't require answers to the myriad questions she had about Christianity before she could put her trust in Jesus by means of a simple faith that He is the risen Son of God. Did she sincerely do and believe all that? Well, one lasting testimony can be found in the following item in her journal:

> I guess to most people religion is a minor issue. Sure, I believe in God, but that's about all it is to them. I know there aren't many people like me, at least not in my school, who take religion seriously. I belong to an excellent Bible church in Hillsdale and I'm a member of the church Youth Group. I'm also one of the five kids out of some thirty members of our Youth Group who's on the planning committee. . . .

Three Saturdays out of a month we have a regular Youth Group meeting. We do a lot of different things at these meetings. We usually have one theme and discuss it the whole night. On Wednesday we have prayer meetings and on Friday we go to movies or bowling or roller skating. But all in all we really have a great time together.

"Maria's approach very often was to put herself second," Walt says. "Once, she had an argument with a boy who had been leading her on. I said to her, 'Why don't you tell him to go jump in a lake?' Maria said she *couldn't* do that. What she said she *was* going to do was pray about the situation. She was a lot deeper spiritually than we had realized and this love she had for the Lord was the most important thing in her life."

After Maria's death, Walt and Connie Van Beers rummaged through their daughter's belongings and, much to their surprise and delight, found that there were many scraps of paper on which she had jotted down all sorts of items. "It turns out that she had a habit of writing down whatever her problem was and then putting down the portion of Scripture that gave her the answer she had obviously been searching through the Bible for," Walt explains.

"From all I've learned since the accident, I think Maria *knew* that she was going to be leaving us and I believe that in some ways she was trying to tell us that. On the way to church one day not long before the accident, we were joking around when all of a sudden she said, 'Dad, what would you ever do if something happened to me and I was killed?' I actually got mad at her and turned around and looked at her and said, *'Don't ever kid about that.'* "

One of Maria's final school assignments was to write a poem about any topic she cared to. This is what she penned two days before her death:

Poem of Own Choice
The morning sun rises
and lightens the sky,
The world once at rest
has awakened.
The day has begun.
People live. People die.
Time passes on forsaken.
Days turn to weeks, months,
    years.

A life once before you is now
the past.
Problems and answers cause
many fears.
How long will you live?
How long does life last?

The piece of notebook paper on which she wrote the original version of that poem contains several thoughts. Beneath what turned out to be the last line of her final draft, Maria scratched out these lines:

What does life mean?
What's the purpose of it all?
There's so much to be seen.
Is there a beginning?
Is there an end?
Does life have a meaning?

There was yet one more line that she wrote, one near the bottom of the page. Oddly, she neither crossed it out nor included it in the version she turned in to her teacher. This was her last line:

Is the end near?

4

Tommy Carroll

His Middle Initial Was E—for Emerson or Maybe Excellent

If he thought highly of something, Thomas Carroll didn't use the expressions more conventional among teenagers: "great" or "super" or "terrific." To be sure, when this bespectacled lefthander was around other youngsters he at least occasionally used those words and even threw in an 'Oh, wow!" now and then, just as his peers did. But "excellent" was *his* word.

Among the things he felt deserved to be called "excellent" were puns, blueberry pie, his mother's chocolate chip cookies, her oatmeal cookies, and the ice cream or soda he would almost always treat himself to at Carvel's while making his newspaper deliveries. Broccoli and turnips, however, were definitely *not* "excellent." Chicken was a rare bird, attaining both high and low marks from Thomas (or Tommy, as all his young friends called him). He enjoyed the taste of chicken, but only after he discarded the skin, which he regarded to be yukkie. Tommy also didn't like getting his hands messy when he picked up a portion of chicken and munched on it.

"He had a saying for that," Martha Carroll remembers with a smile. "Thomas would say, 'You have to use forty-six napkins to eat chicken.' As soon as he finished with the chicken, he'd always head right for the sink to wash off his hands."

Playing the piano was "excellent." So was playing bumper pool in the basement at home. So was riding his blue ten-speed Schwinn bicycle which his dad says, "Had all the extras you could buy for it." So was going for a spin on his four-and-a-half horsepower Rupp minibike with torque converter. And so was having birthday parties because he could share the good times with many of the young people he enjoyed most: nephews and nieces who lived nearby, plus Mark and Brian Hayhurst, and Eric Borloz.

"We gave his piano to Salt and Light," Martha Carroll says as she glances at the far wall of the living room where the upright used to stand. "He was so diligent about his lessons. Not long after he had started playing, we went away for an Easter weekend. Thomas was so concerned about the fact that he might not be able to get in his piano practice that we had to call ahead to the place where we were going to find out if they had a piano there that he could use. He was so relieved to find out that they did.

"I had Thomas when I was forty-four. It's harder in a different way when you're older. You don't have the stamina or the strength you once did. But he was such a joy. The fourteen years he was with us were not easy, but he brought so much joy into our lives. He was worth all the effort, even if we had him only for fourteen years. I think the thing I'll always remember most is that whenever he came into our presence he had that winsome smile. Our daughter's mother-in-law expressed it that way. I had never thought of it like that, but it was true that he always had a smile that said, 'Everything's worthwhile.' That seemed to be his attitude all of his life."

"What I *always* saw in Thomas was joyful enthusiasm," his father says. "He was enthusiastic about everything he did. He rode his bike enthusiastically. Thomas was an avid reader and would read anything he could get his hands on. He ate enthusiastically. He played the piano enthusiastically. The way he did these and many other things, you would have thought that *whatever* he was doing at the moment was the greatest event of his life. It was a joy to see someone with an attitude like that."

Tommy was more restrained when in the company of those his age. Other members of the Pascack Bible Church youth group of 1978 invariably begin their description of him in the same way: "He was quiet." That was understandable. After all, he was only a freshman in high school. And the things he excelled at were not the sort that prompted young people to stand up and cheer. Let's face it, do teenagers snap their heads around to get a glimpse of someone because he or she is a member of the National Junior Honor Society? An outstanding athlete might be accorded such attention. But a straight-A student? That'll be the day. Something else to be faced: Do teenagers or "anyagers" get turned on by a youngster who studies his Bible daily,

Tommy Carroll

memorizes portions of Scripture and tries mightily to develop a consistent prayer life? If they did, Tommy would have turned on many people. As it was, he was gingerly feeling his way through life, trying to find his niche among his peers.

There was a strong indication that he had made up his mind that he was going to assert and express himself when it came to spiritual matters. A few days after going to a movie in Westwood—*Who Is Killing the Great Chefs of Europe?*—Tommy spoke up. Other youngsters who had been in the group that went on the spur of the moment to see the show found no fault with it. Tommy, however, felt there were a few questionable areas. He also felt that, henceforth, much more discretion should be used before going to movies because Christians had an obligation not to be associated in any way with anything immoral or of questionable taste. His point was apparently well made: More than three years later, quite a few youngsters remember how Tommy spoke up. One of them, Bonnie Furman, says of him, "He was so pure."

"He was concerned about the situation and that said a lot to me because he was only a high school freshman," says Randy Miller, who was the youth group leader then. "That night—I believe it was at a Wednesday youth group meeting at church that Tommy spoke up—he also said, 'Let's pray about this. Let's be more careful about screening various things we do. Let's make sure we're a better witness.' Those things said *a lot* to me."

"I always wondered what he was thinking," Pastor Beveridge reveals. "Tom spoke very little, but when he did it was about spiritual matters. He sat on the right-hand side in church, as I looked out at the congregation from the pulpit, and he was always an attentive listener. Often, he had a quizzical grin on his face."

According to Martha Carroll, "Thomas, by his own choice, *had* to be up at six o'clock in the morning to read his Bible. He kept it on the corner of the table next to the recliner."

It was in his father's recliner, a dark red vinyl one, that Tommy would curl up for his morning reading. Before he reached for his Bible, though, he snuggled himself up in a tan afghan-type throw made of synthetic fur. If he hadn't already done so by then, Tommy would put on his glasses. Knowing Tommy, he surely considered this to be an *excellent* way to begin a day.

Tommy, who was remarkably organized and who didn't like to rely solely on his memory, also kept an up-to-date list of items and people to be prayed for. That Tommy was earnest about this was evident from the last such list he compiled:

Things to Pray For

Ran. & Barb [Randy Miller and his wife Barbara had recently separated]
Music Group
Faith Promise
Baptism
Papers (Yes-No)
HiBA people
Piano Practicing (More)
Reading Bible (More)
Spiritual Health (anybody)
Physical   "   (")
Mental   "   (")
Emotional   "   (")
Rebellion against Satan
Homework
School

Bicycle (front derailleur-cable)
Sell Rupp
Dad
Mom
Bill [his brother]
Janet Gaddis
Marty & Sarah Wortman
Outreach
Eric
Mark & Rob [friends Mark Hayhurst and Rob Grieve]
Brian (license) (parallel parking)
gifts

Clearly, Tommy was a young man of strong convictions. Christianity was not merely a fringe element in his life; it was the capstan around which all else revolved. Tommy knew Christ as the friend He was promised to be to all who seek Him earnestly.

There were other sides to him, too. As his father phrases it, "He was a little businessman. Thomas thought of himself as an affluent young man because he was making more than $20 a week from his newspaper route. On his last Father's Day with us, he gave me a nice belt, a reversible black and brown leather one which is the only one I still use."

Martha Carroll also has a gift from her son that she treasures: a half-brown, half-blue ceramic coffee cup that she uses regularly. Among other items the Carrolls cherish are some of Tommy's drawings and writings from when he was in second grade. In a folder containing these materials are a drawing of a girl with pink hair and these two pieces of writing:

My Father

My father has black hair and brown eyes. He owns Carroll's Upholstery Shop. He loses money and earns money. The store is at 89 Westwood Avenue., Westwood, N.J. When he has spare time, he reads the newspaper. He takes us camping. My fathers name is Laurence. I love him very much.

My Mother

My mothers name is Martha Scranton Carroll. She is nice. She cooks very well. She has gray and brown hair. She is very buatiful [not a bad try for a second-grader]. She is fifty-two years old. She is a good bed maker. She is a very good mother. I love her because she is very nice. She goes to work at Father's own store.

Several years later, Tommy completed another school assignment by writing an article entitled, *Mark Hayhurst, My Best Friend.* One of the briefest things he ever wrote is, in retrospect, the most poignant of his writings. The following piece of homework may well have been due the Monday after the accident, because there is no indication that it was given a grade by the teacher. Twelve days before the crash Tommy wrote this for his seventh-period English I class:

My Epitaph

I, Thomas Carroll, died on October 31, 1978 while riding my bike to school. Some pig car driver ran me over while I was turning onto President Road. I was 14.

"Thomas was an odd child in some ways, at least according to what is considered to be the norm," his father points out. "He wanted *so much* to please us. We didn't have to discipline him very much. He gave his mother cards on Valentine's Day. And he was always such a willing worker. He helped out in the store we owned, a furniture and upholstery business in town, and he often went with me when I had deliveries to take care of. People would see this little fella holding on to one end of a big box and they would come running and asking, 'Can I give you a hand?' I would tell those people, 'Sure, take *my* end.' They all wanted to lend a hand because they thought Thomas wasn't very strong, but by the time he was fourteen he had developed quite a bit of strength. If anyone needed help during that last year, it was me. I wasn't feeling well then, but Thomas was getting stronger. He was concerned about my health. For a while, Thomas parked his minibike in front of my store because he was trying to sell it. One day, he had both his bicycle and the Rupp down there and when it came time to go home he pushed the minibike and I pushed his bike. When I tried to get on the bicycle to ride it, I lost my balance and fell on a grassy spot by the sidewalk. I wasn't hurt, but Thomas came over to me and with great concern in his voice asked, 'You all right, Dad?' It wasn't so much *what* he said as it was *how* he said it that revealed how concerned he was about me."

"Thomas was so busy," his mother says. "He was home only one or two nights a week because he was involved in so many activities with the church—Brigade, Bible studies, Salt and Light and other things. When he would come home from school, the first thing he would do was get on his bike, pick up his newspapers from the distributor and then deliver them. He was a busy person, but he wasn't restless. Thomas was a contented person. He couldn't stand getting anything less than an A in school and he never did after he got two Bs when he was in fifth grade. I got annoyed with him for being so busy. It used to bother me that even if he came home as late as midnight, he'd stay up because he had homework that had to be done. He would stay up until he finished it all and then he would be up at six in the morning to read his Bible. I had thought about keeping him home that last day because I knew he had so many things going on. He had to rake the leaves. He had to help Brian with his car. He had lots of homework for the weekend. When I came back from the store, I was going to ask him if he had finished everything. I didn't see how he could have and I thought maybe he should have stayed home to get caught up. But I didn't ask him. Thomas asked Bill if he wanted to go to the meeting that night. Bill sometimes went, but that night he decided he wanted to stay home."

Had Martha Carroll asked Tommy if he had taken care of all his schoolwork, she might have been surprised by his reply and would have found little cause to have grounded him for the evening. The ever-methodical Tommy had jotted down his five homework assignments on a piece of three-ring notebook paper. Here is that list, complete with all his abbreviations:

H-wk

11/10 World Cult—do review sheet *study*
       Bio—rd. chps 4&5
       Spanish—STUDY textbook p. 64A, 76B, 77D
       Geo.—p. 141, 28, 29
       English—do Crossword Puzzle, do notebook

When Tommy completed an assignment, he placed a check mark next to it. Four items were checked off. Only the first on the list wasn't done. If Martha Carroll had known that, she probably would not have felt any strong reason to have kept him home. Perhaps it was because Tommy *was* going home.

Tommy's middle name was Emerson. It was given him by his mother in honor of Thomas Emerson of Ipswich, Massachusetts. Later, the family tree included Ralph Waldo Emerson, who was Tommy's great-grandfather's first cousin. One of the poet's most memable poems was *Threnody,* a title that comes from a Greek word and means a piece of writing that laments something, usually a death. *Threnody* was written by Emerson in 1842 following the death of his six-year-old son Waldo. Near the end of the poem are several lines that seem to be uniquely appropriate at this point. These are the four lines, with the italicized words as Emerson italicized them:

> Voice of earth to earth returned,
> Prayers of saints inly burned,—
> Saying, *What is excellent,*
> *As God lives, is permanent.*

5

Eric Borloz

"The String's Too Heavy"

A photograph of Eric Borloz (the "z" is *not* silent) a few months before the accident shows him with his eyes narrowed, his lips pursed and his chin thrust out. If those facial features could somehow express themselves in words, it would be revealing to hear what they would say. "I've decided to be guided by my beliefs," the eyes would say. "I don't care whether you agree with me or not," the lips would add. "My jaw is ready for you to punch, but I know I'm *right* and there's no way you'll change my mind or beat me into submission," the chin would insist.

Eric wasn't the sort who looked for fights. He had, however, settled his stand on several important issues and he wasn't going to back down, even though he had to pay a dear price for being so unrelenting. To say that he was "stubborn" would be too casual or convenient a description. Yes, there were strains of stubbornness in many things he did. But when someone stands up for his or her viewpoints because they are built upon the convictions of one's heart and mind, then that's far more than being stubborn. That's being decisive, firm. And when one takes that position *knowing* that he or she will be misunderstood and shunned, well, that requires going beyond being decisive and firm. That often calls for nothing short of courage.

The other four youngsters also displayed forms of courage. Mark Hayhurst by going to Honduras. Brian Hayhurst by committing himself to a leadership role. Maria Van Beers by being such an outspoken witness. Tommy Carroll by telling others in the youth group that they should not be so flip about their personal conduct because, above all, they had to keep in mind that they were representing the Lord wherever they went. All four exemplified the strength of their Christian character in other ways. Whether Eric was more courageous than others is not the question to be weighed. It is simply that his kind of courage was less easily comprehended and that, in fairness to him, it is time to clarify who he was and what he stood for.

To get a grasp on *who* Eric was, it is imperative to know *what* he stood for, *why* he did so, *when* he adopted this posture, *where* he took his stand, and *how* he expressed his views. Those who did not know him well probably considered Eric to be a nominal Christian, at best. There were signs, though, that he was more than that. That he had bought a Bible a few months before his death might seem rather inconsequential—until it is realized that Eric had purchased an expensive leather-covered Bible. Although Eric was somewhat free with his money in certain ways, he was not a spendthrift. He was also not impulsive, preferring to give considerable thought to most matters, not the least of which was how he would spend his money. Buying a costly Bible would seem to indicate that Eric intended to make frequent use of that volume. And use it he did. What he learned from his own studies in the Bible, from going to church, from meetings with the youth group, and from conversations with his parents gave Eric distinct guidelines for how Christians should behave.

"When Eric finally accepted the Lord and realized that there was something to the Bible, he felt you had to live according to the way God wanted you to live," Mary Jane Borloz points out. "He tried to live it the way he saw it. When he accepted Christ, it was a *total* thing for him and he was very hurt when he thought that people were not living the way he felt they should. While he was with the youth group on a retreat in Boston two months before he died, Eric had a falling out with some of the kids. Eric fell short, too. We all do. But he was so discouraged because he saw in some of those youngsters the kind of behavior he felt was not right."

"Eric was angry with our group as a whole because of its cliquishness," Craig Cussimanio explains. "He was mad. Eric wanted all of us to be equally close to each other. All groups have some people who enjoy the company of some more than others. But when Eric told us how angry he was, we felt at fault for not trying to reach out more to others. Bob and Jan McCarthy talked to us about the situation and told us, 'We're all brothers and sisters in Christ and we should treat each other as such.'

"Eric wasn't the easiest person to get to know. He would talk to you if you talked to him, or he might say 'Hi' from across the room if you saw him. Sometimes he'd sit like this [arms folded, scowl on face], as if

Eric Borloz

he was saying, 'OK, who's gonna talk with me?' " Throughout his comments about Eric, Craig speaks with tenderness in his voice. The same tone is evident as he continues. "For a while, Eric didn't come to the meetings. Then the McCarthys talked with him and invited him to come back and express his feelings to us. When Eric came back, he seemed to be more comfortable with the group," Craig finishes up, punctuating his words with a momentary faraway look and a slight smile.

"Eric also resented the fact that the others wouldn't accept him for who he was," Mary Jane says. "He refused to work at trying to be recognized. If you don't do something to get recognition, kids just don't pay much attention to you. Eric was quiet and others didn't notice him much. I'm so glad that the McCarthys helped him straighten things out. They apparently helped him understand that he had an obligation to the group, too, and that he would have to get over his hurt and start over. It was just two weeks before he died that Eric decided he had to patch things up and he went back to the youth group."

The church's youth leader, Randy Miller, played a significant role in bringing Eric back to the group, too. "He felt the group had too many cliques, that there was petty backbiting and that there was too much gossip going on," Miller said. "After he'd been away from the meetings for a time I called him up on a Sunday afternoon and told him, 'I'm coming over to get you.' He had to receive permission from his dad to go with me, I remember. Then we went to the church and sat in the parking lot and had a talk. I was telling him that he had to set an example for the other kids and that just because he saw some things wrong in the group was no reason to stop coming to the meetings."

"Eric was a quiet, sensitive youngster," Pastor Beveridge recalls. "He was not a bad-looking boy. I remember he had very dark eyebrows that almost grew together and that he had dark, penetrating eyes. I felt there was a lot of personality lurking underneath the surface but that it was never fully manifested."

How true. Few people knew Eric well. This, as he had come to admit to himself with the help of the McCarthys and Miller, was not entirely other people's fault. Eric was often so quiet that it was easy to overlook him. One of the few close friends he had was Tommy Carroll. When Eric was a sophomore at Westwood High School, Tommy was a freshman. Sensing that Tommy could use some companionship at school and knowing that the two of them shared a love for Christ, Eric made a point of having lunch with him daily.

"Eric was special," his mother says, as well she might. "Don't get me wrong. There were times when you felt like wringing his neck. His favorite expression was, 'Don't worry.' I'd get after him about getting his homework done or about delivering his papers on time. No matter what it was, his reply was always the same, 'Don't worry, Mom. It'll get done.' It *always* did get done. He was also a junk collector. When we cleaned out his room right after the funeral, we found drawers filled with all sorts of junk—pieces of string, gum wrappers (Why would anyone save gum wrappers?), you name it. [Among the 'you-name-its' were nuts and bolts, gears, pieces of wire, scraps of metal, worn-out shoelaces, leaves, scraps of paper, aluminum foil and scads of other items.]

"Eric had said that after he graduated from high school he wanted to wait a year before going to college. He wasn't sure if he wanted to go or what he might want to study. And he said, 'Why spend $5,000 or more a year if I'm not sure that I really want to go to college?' If Eric was turned on by a teacher or a course, he always got good grades. One year he had a social studies teacher he didn't like and he got C's in the course. The next time he had social studies, he thought the teacher was terrific and Eric got A's. He had an incredible sensitivity about people. The thing that touched me most after his death was the inscription under the picture they had of him in the high school yearbook the next spring."

In the 1979 edition of *Crossroads,* the school yearbook, there were photos of Tommy, Eric, Mark, and Brian, with a verse of Scripture beneath each. Below the picture of Eric were these words from John 14:3 (New International Version).

> And if I go and prepare a place for you, I will come back and take you to be with me that you also may be where I am.

Howard Borloz, like his wife, found that Eric could be exasperating at times. One classic instance had to do with a kite. Howard tells the story this way: "He was determined that this kite, which he had built himself, should fly. The fact that there wasn't sufficient wind to bring about the proper aerodynamics to get the kite airborne was not going to deter him. His primary thought was: 'I built the kite, therefore it *must* fly. It *will* fly.' So we went out to a field to see if it would fly. There were slight gusts of wind, but not enough to keep the kite aloft. After endless futile attempts, I said, 'Eric, there is not enough wind.' He said, 'No, Dad. The problem is that the string's too heavy.' We went through it a few more times and then I, in desperation, said, 'We are going home because there isn't enough wind.' He accepted the fact that we were going home. But in his mind we were going home 'because the string's too heavy.' The next time he took the kite out, he replaced the string he had been using with nylon fishing line. It was a pretty windy day, and his kite flew well. He said the reason for the success was the nylon fishing line. He never would acknowledge the fact that the kite might have flown better because it was considerably windier that day. That was Eric. If he *wanted* to do something, he would put his mind to it and he would get it done."

Eric's stubbornness and his "don't worry" philosophy understandably irritated his parents at times. He more than compensated for those quirks with his generosity, which extended to members of his family and well beyond. Bringing goodies to the Salt and Light sessions was only a small part of his bigheartedness.

"When long hair was in, Eric found that he needed a hair dryer to get his hair dried quickly after he washed it," Mary Jane says. "So he bought a hair dryer. About a week later, his brother Andy came home from college and thought that the hair dryer was really neat. 'If you like it, you can have it,' Eric told Andy, who took it back to school with him. That's the way Eric was. I had to be careful around him that I didn't mention that I'd seen something that I wished I had. If I did, he'd go right down and buy it for me.

"Another example of his generosity was the night he and Mark Hayhurst went from Salt and Light to a local pizza parlor. While they were there, a young man who had phoned in an order for a pizza came in to pick it up. He had to wait for his order and while he did he ordered a slice of pizza that he could eat right there. Then he discovered he didn't have enough money to pay for everything. Eric went to him and gave him whatever the amount was that the man was short. The young man asked him why he had done that and Eric told him it was because he was a Christian and he wanted to help out. Well, this *really* opened things up. The young man started asking the boys about their Christianity. They went on and on, and the man had many questions, some of which got quite deep. Finally, the boys took him over to Salt and Light, where there were some older people in charge who were better able to answer those questions."

"Whatever he bought, he had to buy with money he had earned, because I never gave him any," Howard adds. "His main job was delivering papers. That was our father-and-son thing. On weekends, I'd get in the van with Eric and we'd go pick up the papers, get them ready and deliver them.

"He always did a good job on his paper route, largely because we taught him what to do and insisted that he do it correctly. His tips were fantastic. He had about sixty customers and one Christmas he got $240 in tips. There were times when he would be late getting home from delivering his papers. Sometimes it was because he had stopped in to help someone who needed a hand with something. Other times it was because he was a good listener and people found they could talk to him about all kinds of things. One woman used to pour out her problems to him. My first thought when I heard about this was, 'What good would it be for a middle-aged woman to be telling her troubles to an adolescent? What could Eric do except listen sincerely?' I guess that might have been helpful, though. I know I always told him, 'God gave you two ears, two eyes and one mouth. That's because He intended for you to do a lot of listening, a lot of watching and a little talking.' "

"There were a number of times when people would mention things to me that they thought I knew all about but which I didn't," Mary Jane points out. "When they realized I didn't know what they were talking about, they would say they had mentioned it to Eric and they were sure he had told me all about whatever it was. Then I'd ask Eric about it and he would tell me he hadn't mentioned those things to me because those people had asked him to be quiet about them."

Aside from his newspaper deliveries, Eric earned money by shoveling snow off people's sidewalks and driveways. What those neighbors didn't realize was that for much of the winter of 1977-78 he shoveled with a broken right arm. Eric broke the arm while on a retreat with the youth group to upstate New York, where he was injured while hurtling down a steep hill in an inner tube. Although his arm hurt, it was not until the weekend was over and he returned home that he had the arm checked by a doctor. Hardly had his arm been placed in a cast before it began to snow. Heeding his call to duty rather than to the throbbing pain he felt, Eric grabbed his shovel and went to work.

"Eric was definitely not into sports," Mary Jane says. "He was going to go out for cross-country, but I think that was mostly because he was so impressed with Mr. Dietz, who was his teacher for mechanical drawing as well as the coach for the sport. For a while, Eric went to the track every morning and ran. It wasn't long before he came down with knee trouble. Eric just wasn't a runner. He seemed to run in the same place too long and not get anywhere. The only other sport he wanted to get involved with in high school was wrestling. He had decided to try out for the team and had bought weights and a bench to build himself up. But he hardly had a chance to use the stuff before he was killed."

For someone who "was definitely not into sports," Eric did quite well. Every Thursday for years he went to the local police rifle range and practiced target shooting. Eric, who had taken courses in safety and shooting techniques, earned a batch of badges and medals for his marksmanship. He also took part in a Pinewood Derby race. His father had helped the older Borloz boys—Steven and Andy—build racers to enter Derbies years before. Andy finished second the year he competed.

"It was a matter of progression, learning from one racer to the next,"

Howard says. "By the time we put Eric's together, we were able to benefit from our experience. And, by George, Eric came in first. What he enjoyed more than anything, though, was his minibike. He used to ride it all the time in Gritman Park, which is right near our house. Eric bought the tubular frame and all the parts separately, and then he assembled it himself. He was pretty good mechanically and could do anything he put his mind to."

That he could. When Eric decided he wanted to learn how to build a ship in a bottle, he got a book about the subject, studied and before long the Borlozes had two bottles containing ships. When an old sewing machine went on the fritz, Eric repaired the motor, which he had planned to rig up so that he could activate a moving target to fire his BB gun at.

"At times, he displayed the kind of engineering acumen that would have delighted my father," Howard says. "If you are familiar with portable window air conditioners, you know that they are awkward to handle. It's not that they are so heavy. It's just that it takes a certain amount of dexterity, not necessarily great strength, to install one. I came home from work one day and saw that the air conditioner was in the window of Eric's room. 'How did he get it in all by himself?' I asked Mary Jane. It turned out that he had used some ingenuity. What he did was to get a ladder and place it near the window. Then he got a scaffolding plank, which he braced on one of the ladder rungs and on the window sill so that the plank would be level. After that, he went to his room, picked up the air conditioner and put it in place without having to worry that it might fall out of the window before he got it properly in place.

"He also rigged up a photoelectric cell and a beeper in his room. That way, if the dog [Sammy] came into Eric's room he would break the electric beam and set off the noise that would scare him off. One Christmas, he bought an electric cookie gun for his mother because she always makes so many cookies at that time of year. Eric became intrigued with it when he learned that the cookie gun could also be used to make cream puffs. When Mary Jane was supposed to make cream puffs for some event, Eric was the one who made them with the electric cookie gun. To understand Eric, you have to appreciate that he did this not necessarily because he liked cream puffs, but *because he had a machine that could make them.*

"He was unique. I mean, when we asked Eric what he wanted for a gift one year he said he wanted a carbide lamp. We had to look for a long time before we found one. Why he wanted a carbide lamp I never knew. When he bought himself a watch, he bought a pocket watch. How many young boys would rather carry around a pocket watch than wear a wristwatch?"

Eric's eating habits were typical of teenagers. Vegetables seldom made it from his dinner plate to his mouth, much to his mother's dismay. Ice cream, pizza and hoagies, however, were devoured with consummate joy. Eric often rode his bicycle a mile from his house to the Baskin-Robbins ice cream parlor on Broadway in Westwood. After buying a pint—many times it was a quart—of ice cream, he would pedal home and devour it all by himself. If he didn't do that he would go into one of his pizza routines.

"Along about nine o'clock at night he would say, 'Hey, Dad, how about a pizza?' I'd say, 'fine.' Then he'd call up, order a pizza to be delivered to the house by Angelo's. Eric would pay for it and give the delivery boy a tip. Then we'd all have pizza. He thought it was a great thing to be able to treat us that way. Lots of times he made his own pizza. Eric made them out of everything you could think of. As long as he could find some spaghetti sauce and cheese, he would find a way to make a pizza. He made pizzas out of English muffins, slices of bread, even crackers if he had nothing else. His other thing was to go out every Saturday and buy himself one of those big heroes. That was about a three-dollar sandwich. I would say to him, 'But son, your mother has lunch at home for you that won't cost you a cent.' Then I thought about it all and realized that at least he was spending his money on something he enjoyed and that this was a lot better than the things many kids his age were spending money on."

Obviously, Eric did not go through life with his eyes narrowed, his lips pursed and his chin thrust out. He was fast becoming his own man, one of high principles, determination, self-reliance and whims that he exercised much to his own delight and that of his family. That he was a giving, sharing, loving person reflects much upon his parents, who passed on to him many of the virtues that he put into practice. There is no finer example of the warmth within the family than the following, which Howard Borloz relates:

"Eric and I had a routine that we went through for years each morning that I had to go to work. Although I had to leave rather early, Eric would be out of bed at 6:15 to see me off. Before I left, I would say to him, 'Remember son, I love you and the *Lord* loves you.' Then I would get in the car to drive to work. Before I drove off, I always turned back and looked at Eric, who was standing in the doorway. Then I would wave to him and drive off. To this day, I *always* turn around and look for him. For a long time, I would wave, too. Now I may not always wave but I *always* look back."

6

The Salt and Light Company

Bob McCarthy and his wife Jan were in charge of Salt and Light from its inception in February of 1978 until they moved to Florida in mid-1979. "One day, we were talking with Pastor Beveridge about where we could meet with this group so we could become more involved with them," Jan recalls. "Pastor said, 'What you need is a storefront ministry.' All of a sudden something clicked and I could feel tears starting to flow. Bob looked at me and said, 'The basement of our store. We've been praying about what to do with it.'"

The McCarthys had recently begun a business called Frame It Yourself, a picture-framing enterprise. "I was going to use the downstairs as a place where artists could display their work," Bob points out. "But the morning we talked with Fred, a storefront ministry seemed like the best use for the place. Pastor said, 'We'll call it the Salt and Light Company.'"

Pastor Beveridge later explained why he chose this name, saying, "I've been impressed by the figures of penetration that the Lord used in Matthew 5, where He describes Christians as 'the salt of the earth' and 'the light of the world.' In *The Company of the Committed*, Elton Trueblood stresses the importance of salt, light, and other forms of penetration used in the Bible. These figures of penetration have always been dear to me because I think they represent what committed Christianity really is."

"It was either that Sunday or the next that we took the kids after church, loaded them into a bus, drove into town, and went to look at the basement," Bob McCarthy continues. "The place was filled with junk, but I asked the kids, 'Could you envision this as a place that Christ could use?' They said they could. So we formed a circle, prayed, and dedicated the basement to the Lord. Most of those who helped clean the place and fix it up had graduated from high school already.

The five were from a younger age bracket, but soon they began joining in and coming to the meetings.

"Of all the kids who came, the five were the most faithful. They were there *every* Friday night and they became the real core of the group. Brian, who was the oldest of the five, came with his brother Mark and they helped get the basement ready. Mark was very interested in people. 'What's going on with you?' he'd ask and then he'd get into conversation with somebody. There were some rivalries between Mark and Brian about things. Having his younger brother in the same group sometimes bugged Brian. *Both* of them were bugged when the oldest Hayhurst boy—David—would come home from college and attend the meetings.

"Brian and Maria were the organizers. He was a 'What're-we-gonna-do-next?' type. Not that Brian wanted nothing but activities. He wanted very much to see friendships develop among the group. Maria was the kind of person who could rally people, get them sparked up. She wouldn't let people frown for long. When Maria came to the meetings, she often brought along some girls from Upper Saddle River, which is where she lived.

"Tommy was the youngest, shortest and shiest of the five. His father owned the building where our Frame It Yourself business was located and Tommy got a big kick out of remembering how he used to work with his dad in the basement that was now the meeting place for Salt and Light. He used to look around and say, 'I *can't believe* this is my father's old place.' Tommy was *so* cooperative and he *loved* to laugh so much.

"During the first week of November of '78, Eric came to us and said he'd made a breakthrough with a problem he'd had for a long time. He made us promise that we wouldn't tell anyone what it was, but we can say that we were thrilled that Eric had come to us for help and that he now knew an inner healing had taken place. Eric was a very giving person—not just of material things, but of his life. He responded quickly to any type of love or affection and he gave back a lot in those areas. Eric made a dove out of wood during shop class at school, painted the name of Jesus on it and brought it to one of our meetings. We hung it up on one of the walls and it's been there ever since. Friday after Friday, Eric would bring goodies and when we'd ask, 'Hey, where did these potato chips and pretzels come from?' he'd just smile.

"The five brought lots of other youngsters to Salt and Light and some of them made commitments to Christ," says Bob. "Our attendance was usually in the teens, but we'd get up as high as sixty on nights when we had a musical group or a good movie. The makeup of the group changed during the night because kids would leave and others would come in. At first, that was frustrating. Then I realized Salt and Light was becoming a comfortable place for lots of youngsters who found they weren't being threatened by a church. Friday wasn't a Bible time or a study time. It was just a chance for the kids to fellowship among themselves and to have a good time."

All five were at the Salt and Light gathering on November 10th. Eric, as usual, made sure he was one of the first to arrive so that he could, without fanfare, put out the bags of pretzels and potato chips he had bought. As Tommy Carroll got ready to go to the meeting, he would have liked to have slid down the banister and into the foyer of his house. The high gloss on that railing was a result of innumerable such descents by Tommy. This night, though, he disdained such a joy ride, most likely because he knew his frame was at long last beginning to fill out and that he had probably outgrown trips on the banister.

Mark Hayhurst's failure to get his long blond hair cut had nearly kept him from going to Salt and Light that evening. "He was supposed to have had it cut the previous weekend," his father says. "Mark kept pushing it and pushing it. When he got home that night from collecting money for his paper route, he began hurrying around the house. I asked him why he was in such a rush and he said he was going to Salt and Light. I reminded him that, according to our rules, he was grounded for the entire weekend because he still hadn't had his hair cut. 'I called the barber and he told me he was all booked up tonight but that he'd take me first thing tomorrow morning,' Mark told me. 'I thought that'd be all right.' I really wanted him to go to the meeting because it was always such a blessing. So I said, 'OK, I'll buy that.' "

That was all Mark had to hear. Within minutes, he and Brian were out the door in their typical fashion—that is to say, like a pair of stampeding buffaloes. At the meeting, Brian and Mark told Tommy and Eric their help would be needed the next afternoon on one of the most critical phases of their big project. This venture had been going on for months and involved extensive repairs to an old Karmann-Ghia that reposed in the Hayhurst garage. Saturday's goals: hoist the engine back into place and get the car running after months of being idle.

Maria Van Beers had no such interest in automotives. She did, though, have an interest in two of the young mechanics. Such feelings were, in a few instances, starting to emerge from that marvelous cocoon of teenage secrecy about tender matters of this sort. It may have hurt Maria somewhat when she noticed that two people left the Salt and Light meeting for a while: one of her dearest girlfriends, a teenager she had brought into the youth group herself—Laurie Cole—and the boy she loved the most—Brian Hayhurst. In recent weeks, Maria had come to accept this situation and, if anything, she probably appreciated it that Laurie and Brian did not make open displays of their mutual affections that night and that they simply went for a hand-in-hand walk through the streets of Westwood.

For Maria, this evening was the start of an especially significant fourteen days that she was genuinely excited about. Her schedule: Salt and Light on the 10th and 17th; Bible studies on the 11th and 18th; roller skating with the youth group on the 13th; her 16th birthday on the 15th; her baptism on the evening of Sunday the 19th; and Thanksgiving on the 23rd.

It was not surprising that the five were drawn to each other or that they formed the heart of the youth group, for they were all sincere about their love for Christ. When Mark had come home from Honduras, he had a dark tan (it didn't last) and a heartfelt certainty about God's love for him and all people (this *did* last). Both Brian and Eric were displaying more and more evidence that they were learning what it meant to put Christ at the center of their lives. When any of these three boys had a question about the Bible, they would sometimes bring it to Tommy. That was because Tommy, who was nicknamed "Preacher" by his friends, was already unusually well-versed in the Scriptures. All five were developing sensitivities about the needs of others and they often reached out to put their faith into practice. When Tom Cussimanio, a friend of the Van Beers family, cut himself badly with a chainsaw, Maria didn't merely send him a get-well card while he was hospitalized; she also sent along Bible verses she felt would be appropriate. Maria was a sophomore at Northern Highlands Regional High School in Allendale. The four boys all lived farther south in Westwood and attended Westwood Regional High School, where Tommy and Mark were freshmen, Eric was a sophomore and Brian was a junior.

More than anything, they were teenagers blessed with the distinctive energies of youth. Each had traits that exasperated their parents or other people. Eric had a streak of stubbornness worthy of a mule. Tommy's jam-packed schedule of activities concerned his folks. Some of Mark's needling stung a few people. Brian's argumentativeness could become wearisome. Maria had a strong will and, when she felt it necessary to get her way, could become pushy. In October of 1978 she wrote the following in a journal she kept:

> I've been having some problems recently with some friends and with my family, and I've really been in a bad mood this past week.... I hate when I get in these moods. No one can tolerate me. I'm always kinda touchy and snappy and, of course, that always makes things worse. But I hope sooner or later these problems will clear up and I'll get out of this lousy mood.

They all had rough edges. Each, though, seemed well aware of those flaws. What was most significant was that they all were making efforts to get rid of those rough spots. Eric had recently demonstrated his willingness to admit that his stubbornness was getting in his own way at times. Tommy did his best to assuage his parents' concern about his busyness by trying to prove that he could handle his paper route, church activities, chores around the house and homework, and still get straight A's in school. Since returning from Honduras, Mark had shown more concern about people's needs. Learning that he was a capable and respected worker may have been why Brian was feeling more self-confident and less inclined to argue. Maria, as her journal entry indicated, was attempting to master her powerful personality so that she would be less disturbing to others and to herself. All five were at work trying to make better people of themselves. Like stones being constantly washed by a river's flowing waters, they were in the process of having their rough edges worn away so they could be what God intended them to be: five smooth stones.

7

Saturday Fever

Pastor Beveridge had theological implications in mind when he spoke about the penetrating qualities of salt and light. At Friday's session of the Salt and Light Company, however, the most penetrating item for much of the night was the same as always at these meetings—laughter.

There was Brian Hayhurst, who seemed to be standing a bit taller than usual in the past few weeks. Perhaps it was because he had recently attained one of youth's most treasured status symbols—a driver's license. There was his brother Mark, laughing gleefully while a needled victim struggled for a quick retort. Enjoying the repartee to the fullest was Tommy Carroll, his head thrown back as he was convulsed by laughter. Eric Borloz appeared to be more at ease than he often was, mingling more freely than he normally did and delighting in the way the food that he had furnished was being devoured—particularly by the ravenous Hayhursts. He didn't exactly seem to mind it that Beth Robertson chatted with him. Eric, who never had much to say at these meetings, spent an entire hour gabbing with Beth. When not engrossed in conversation or laughter, Maria Van Beers managed to keep tabs on just about everybody. This vigil was part of her effort to try to make certain that a good time was had by all and to see if the regular attenders were breaking away from their cliques to mingle with others, especially any newcomers.

"Everyone seemed to have an exceptionally good time," Bob McCarthy remembers. It had been a difficult and poignant day for McCarthy, one he was able to share in some detail with the group that night. McCarthy points out that, "During a bit of a devotional time, I told the kids, 'I've just come from a friend's funeral. His name was Dooley. He was only 27 years old. Dooley was an alcoholic who was separated from his wife and three children. He had a broken leg and was on crutches. He was waiting for a subway in New York a few days

71

ago when, according to witnesses, he apparently lost his balance and fell in front of a train.

" 'I had met him several years ago at a meeting, in New York, where I gave my Christian testimony to drug addicts and alcoholics. When I gave an invitation for those who heard me to accept Christ, only one hand went up. It was Dooley's. He was sincere about coming to Jesus, but the Lord kept reminding me that Dooley needed help, that he still had his ghetto head and that he still had temptations to face. The Lord let me walk alongside Dooley for three, four years, through a lot of hellish times, terrifying times. The Lord had matched us up even though we were an odd couple: Dooley was black; I'm white. Dooley was my entrance into the black community in Manhattan and he gave me an opportunity to present Christ in places where he took me. Dooley introduced me and told people why I was there. Only eternity will tell how many people came to know the Lord because of Dooley's bizarre way of witnessing for Jesus. He himself showed little spiritual growth. But he *really* loved the Lord. I gained a lot spiritually from knowing him. Today I had the privilege of saying a few words at his funeral. Dooley's with the Lord in heaven now. Some day, you kids will meet him there.' "

"When Bob finished talking, Maria made a request," Jan McCarthy says. "Maria had heard about a tape made by a woman who had been dead for twenty-eight minutes [Betty Malz] and she wanted to know if we would play it at the next week's meeting. We promised we would."

Brian and Timmy Biscaye missed part of that night's session. "We took off for a while to go to the Valley Bible Chapel, which is in Washington Township, a few miles from Westwood," Timmy explains. "Their youth group was meeting that night, too, and we just liked the girls there better. Brian also drove around for awhile, just cruising up and down Old Hook Road. We were best friends and did a lot of things together. One day when nobody was home at my place, Brian came over to ice skate on a rink that we had in the backyard. While we skated, we smoked cigars. We made sure not to drop any ashes on the rink because it would have given us away."

After the Salt and Light session broke up, Maria topped off the night by sleeping at the home of her best friend, Beth Robertson, in Allendale. Before trundling off to bed, both girls had some of the cherry pie that had been baked by Mary Robertson, Beth's mother, who knew it was Maria's favorite. When they got up on Saturday morning, they found that Beth's pet gerbil had died in its cage.

"I didn't want to pick it up," Beth Robertson says. "Maria put it in a box and got rid of it. After that, we talked about whether animals go to heaven and then the talk broadened out to people. Maria said she was not worried about dying."

Before Connie Van Beers picked up her daughter that afternoon, Maria wrote a note to Beth's mother thanking her for the cherry pie. Once home, Maria couldn't help noticing all the leaves on the lawn in front of her house. She and a bunch of her friends would some day have to get around to raking those leaves, a job that was part of the youth group's Slave Day project. Slave Day, which was more than a single-day endeavor, was a way for the youngsters to earn money to pay for a retreat they were to go on in February at Camp of the Woods in Speculator, New York. Brian Hayhurst was the so-called Slave Day "master," and he had to coordinate all the logistics for the project as well as keep detailed financial records. Walter Van Beers, Maria's father, had agreed to hire a number of "slaves"—his daughter, Brian, Mark, Eric, Tommy, and possibly Beth and Laurie—to rake the leaves off his lawn. It was no soft-touch negotiator that Walt Van Beers had to go up against when it came to fixing the wages he would have to pay for this raking. Handling the bargaining for the Slave Day group was none other than Maria.

"How much are we going to get paid?" Maria asked her father.

"How does fifteen dollars sound?" Walt asked.

"That doesn't sound too good," replied Maria as she began her push to squeeze out a few more bucks.

"How much do you feel the job is worth?" inquired her dad.

"I'd like you to pay about thirty dollars for the work," Maria said.

"No," Walt responded. *"That* doesn't sound too good."

Back and forth went the negotiations. When an agreement had been hammered out, the price tag had been set at $20. Walt had decided—and Maria probably suspected as much of her generous and easy-going dad—that, "If the kids did a good job I'd give them twenty-five dollars."

Brian, John Hartman, Jr., and Timmy Biscaye, fellow juniors at Westwood High School, were at the local library that morning. (Some libraries were closed because it was Veterans' Day, but the one in Westwood was open.) The three were completing research for a report that was due the following week for their U.S. Diplomacy class.

While they were in the library, Don Hayhurst came in to tell his son that a woman had phoned saying that whoever was to have cleaned her windows had not done so. This did not surprise Brian, who was learning that his role as supervisor of Slave Day meant that he sometimes had to be less of a master and more of a slave. Brian had to keep track of the jobs that people from the church wanted done, determine who had the time and who was best suited to handle each task, note down the hours each member of his crew worked, and record how much money everyone earned. Such record-keeping, Brian felt, was rather neat. What was upsetting was when Brian found that his meticulously prepared schedule was sometimes knocked askew. There were occasions when he would give someone an assignment and the person would tell him, "Sure. I'll clean Mrs. Humpledinker's attic on Saturday morning. You can count on me." Alas, there were times when Brian learned he *couldn't* count on someone. It didn't happen often, but there were instances when Brian or his dad would get a call from a Mrs. Humpledinker that, "Nobody's come to clean my attic." It took some scrambling that Saturday, but with Timmy's assistance, Brian cleaned the windows that one of his workers had forgotten about. First, though, he had to go home and put some ladders in the Hayhursts' red and white Volkswagen van so the windows could be reached. Then Brian picked up Henry Van Der Werf and drove him and Johnny Hartman to Upper Saddle River so they could take care of *their* Slave Day task that afternoon—washing a car.

For Eric, the late morning and early afternoon were devoted mainly to puttering around the house. Tommy helped Don Hayhurst take a load of debris to the town dump and then busied himself at home. Before his mother went to downtown Westwood shortly after noon to help her husband at his furniture and upholstery business, she firmly told Tommy he had to rake the leaves off the front lawn and complete his homework. Time, he therefore knew, could not be wasted. The leaves may have wondered what hit them when Tommy manned his rake with vigor and vengeance. Next in the line of his attack were his school books.

As for Mark, he hurried to the barber shop early that morning. It wasn't that he wanted to get spruced up to play his sax in the high school band when Westwood played at Pascack Hills High School in Montvale that afternoon. What propelled him more than anything was the realization that if he failed *again* to get his hair snipped, he would not be allowed to attend the Bible study that evening. It was a sun-splashed day, with the temperature rising to an unseasonable 61°. Fine weather for playing the saxophone outdoors. Fine weather for a foot-

ball game. (Mark played well. His team did not, losing 35-0.) By the
time Mark returned home, it was late afternoon and he was late joining a handful of boys who had showed up at the garage behind the
Hayhurst house.

Those boys were there to lend their muscles and their fragments of
expertise to Brian, who had asked them to help get the engine back in
the Karmann-Ghia. By the appointed hour—3 P.M.—four boys had
come to lend a hand, a wrench or—as it turned out—a backside:
Tommy Carroll, Eric Borloz, Rob Grieve, and Timmy Biscaye. (Bill
Carroll, Tommy's sixteen-year-old brother, arrived later.) On their
way back from taking care of their Slave Day chores, Brian and
Timmy had purchased a bagful of goodies for everyone to munch and
sip on.

The engine was awkward to manipulate so that it could be installed
properly. By golly, though, those youngsters got it in. A little ingenuity
helped. What those boys did was to tie a sturdy rope around the engine
and then to a tree nearby. Four of the boys (Rob, Timmy, Tommy,
and Mark) then sat on the rope and were thus able to suspend the engine in place while Eric and Brian did most of the tinkering. After the
engine was all hooked up, there came the big test: Would the car start?
It would not. The only thing the boys could determine was that the
problem was with the wiring. It was a dilemma they were unable to
solve before dinnertime.

Mark had shifted his attention from the car to painting the outside
of the garage. His goal was to get one side painted far enough down so
that his father, who was not particularly fond of climbing ladders any
longer, would be able to finish the job with ease. Such industriousness
was to be admired. It was by the light of lamps that were hooked up as
close to the garage as possible so that Mark would be able to see what
he was doing. When the mission was accomplished, Mark and Brian
hurried into the house and jostled one another as they lustily jockeyed
for position at the kitchen sink so they could wash their hands. When
they got done with their elbowing and washing, Mark and Brian
snapped their towels at each other with such force that they sent a
shower of nap through the kitchen. After the combat had subsided,
Don saw Brian standing alone, went to him, cupped his son's face in
his hands and told him with all the sincerity he could muster, "You're
a good boy. Bless you."

Gulping down their dinner left the boys with enough time to make a
phone call to their brother David, who was a sophomore at Rutgers

University. It was with much enthusiasm in their voices that they told David that the motor was back in the car and that, with luck, they'd have it purring before long. There was also just enough time for a changing of clothes, a hair combing and then—like a flash—it was out the door. Brian was the first out. There, pacing the sidewalk in front of the house, was Tommy Carroll, who had accepted an invitation from Brian to ride to the Bible study at Randy Miller's apartment.

Randy's apartment was no more than a ten-minute walk away, but Brian had been thrust into the position of having to drive that night. Actually, he didn't *have* to drive. But at the Wednesday youth meeting, Craig Cussimanio had said that he wouldn't be able to use his family's van to drive youngsters home after the Saturday study. Craig, a youth-group regular, explained that everything had suddenly and un-expectedly fallen into place so that he could make a trip to Syracuse University to help him decide whether or not he wanted to enroll there the following year. No sooner had Craig expressed his apologies for not being able to fulfill his usual role as a driver than Brian piped up, "That's OK, I'll drive." *Of course* he would drive. Hey, he was a proud new licensed motorist and being able to drive his friends around was a heady sensation. Mark, who was also going to ride with Brian, was stopped by his mother just before he could go out the front door. She gave him a once-over to make certain his clothes were neat enough before allowing him to depart. When Mark yanked the front door open, his father, standing on the staircase that led from the foyer to the second floor, could hear the engine of the VW van. Then Mark closed the door and he, Tommy, and Brian were off.

Eric nibbled at his dinner, preferring to pore over a book about automechanics in an effort to try to solve the riddle of why Brian's car wouldn't start. When he left for the mile walk to the Bible study, Eric took the manual with him so that he might be able to glance at it with some of the other boys. Surely, it was a pleasant walk. The night air was surprisingly warm for November, but what Eric must have en-joyed most was thinking about the good things that had happened to him in the past few days. Other people, adults and teens alike, had reached out to him; his prayers were being answered and he saw Christians reacting with the love he had been longing to know. Eric may well have been aware of a sense of newness as he walked, a fresh start with the youth group now that he had patched things up with other youngsters, and a fresh start with the Hayhursts in particular. The Hayhurst boys, with whom he hadn̹'t always been on the best of terms, had invited Eric to help with the car. That was really something. That signified that Brian and Mark wanted to sincerely welcome him back to the youth group.

For the 11th, the youth-group calendar for November 1978 read as follows: MEETING 7:30 AT LAURIE'S. A late change had been made, however. Laurie Cole had considered asking that the Bible study be held elsewhere because a friend of hers was going to be visiting her, but then she felt that wasn't sufficient reason for having the meeting shifted. But when Laurie's sister Cindy became ill on Thursday, Laurie called Randy and reluctantly suggested that the Bible study not be at her house. Randy agreed and quickly spread the word that the meeting would be at his apartment on Center Street in downtown Westwood, right across the street from Frame It Yourself and the Salt and Light headquarters. Laurie opted to stay at home with her guest.

The first at Randy's place were Beth and Maria, who had arranged to have a special dinner with him at the apartment. Maria, whose culinary skills consisted of not much more than making toast and boiling water, had enlisted her mother and younger sister Donna to prepare much of the meal. Donna baked an apple pie. Connie Van Beers concocted a tasty sauce for the lasagna. Maria and Beth, who had been picked up at two that afternoon from the Robertsons by Mrs. Van Beers, boiled the long, flat strips of pasta. The two girls assembled the sauce, pasta, meat, and cottage cheese in a pan and put it in the oven to bake. They also prepared a loaf of garlic bread. When the girls cleared out of the kitchen, Connie had a chance to quickly reflect on the afternoon of baking and laughing, girl talk and tomato sauce, voices that were loud and moments that were soft. For Connie Van Beers, who had only in the past year or so achieved the sort of closeness with Maria that she had longed for, this time together had been treasurable. It was so satisfying for her to realize that not all the warmth in the kitchen had come from the stove.

Maria's sixteenth birthday was not until Thursday of the next week, but Donna could not wait to give her sister an album of music she was anxious to have. "We had gone shopping the night before to get things for Maria's birthday," Connie remembers. "On Saturday, Donna kept saying, 'I'm going to give Maria that record today. I want her to have it *today.*' She did. While we were all busy in the kitchen on Saturday, the record was playing."

Between 5 and 5:15 P.M. Connie dropped Beth and Maria off at

Randy Miller's apartment. Somewhere between Randy's first and second helpings of lasagna, the girls told him the reason they had wanted to have this dinner: Maria and Beth were to be baptized a week from Sunday (as were Tommy and Brian) and they wanted to know if he would perform the service. Several other youngsters were to be baptized, all by Pastor Beveridge.

It was understandable why the girls asked Miller to baptize them. Randy was 23 years old at the time. He was in tune with the world in which teenagers lived, with their music, their lingo. And it surely didn't hurt that Miller was boyishly handsome. Perhaps the most important reason, though, was that the girls wanted to convey to Randy some of their love, concern, and respect at a time when they felt he needed that. Randy's wife had left him a few weeks before. He had shed many tears. Some members of the youth group felt helpless as they observed Miller's grief. What could they do, though? Maria and Beth knew that asking Miller to baptize them wouldn't end his pain, but they at least wanted to reach out.

Miller, who grew up in Oakland, California, had attended church regularly since the age of six or seven. As he puts it, "I gave my life to Christ every Sunday—until I understood all you had to do was ask Him into your life once and that from there on it was a growing experience. The Missionary Alliance Church I went to in Oakland had a highly successful youth group called Omega. We had about 150 members. I saw a lot of people in my circle come to know the Lord. People I never thought would come were coming—longhairs, athletes, troublemakers. *Everything* I did was with that youth group and I learned how important it was to have Christian fellowship. I learned it even more when our family moved to Boston during my senior year of high school because up there we couldn't find the sort of fellowship we had been so used to. Although I'd pretty much grown up in the church, I'd always been aware of the pull of the outside world. In Massachusetts, the fellowship was missing and I started drinking and smoking. I retained my intellectual relationship with the Lord, but I wasn't walking with Him. Then we found a Bible-preaching church, the Westwood Evangelical Free Church right outside of Boston. Pastor Beveridge was the pastor of that church.

"It was after my junior year in college that I decided that I wanted to go into the youth ministry. Pastor Fred helped me a lot. Pascack Bible Church, of which he had become pastor, had recently budgeted money to help a seminary student get by. He even found a school not too far from the church that seemed perfect for me, Alliance Theological Seminary in Nyack, New York." Miller enrolled and began serving as the youth minister for Pascack Bible Church on a part-time basis in May 1977.

Saturday's Bible study was more than the name implied. It was also a time for laughs and songs and for just enjoying being with one another. It was, by all accounts, a thoroughly pleasant evening for Miller, for Betty Grieve (a young adult who did much work with the youth group), and for the nine youngsters who attended: the five plus Beth, Timmy, Rob Grieve, and Henry Van Der Werf. Brian, who had brought along the financial records for Slave Day and for the youth group as a whole, went over those matters with Rob, his helper.

"Randy and I pretended we were playing the piano," Timmy says. "I was the showoff, the loudmouth of the youth group. I used to make fun of Maria because she was Polish. [Van Beers, a Dutch name, comes from Walt's stepfather. Walt's father was Polish.] We had a stormy friendship and made lots of fun of each other. I apologized to her a couple times earlier, but that night I made a *conscious effort* to be friendly toward her, for some reason."

The discord between the two had bothered Maria. The following, complete with a few lines borrowed from here and there, was written a few days earlier by Maria:

Situation Between Me & Tim

Guard well your tongue from careless words,
Whatever else you do:
And ere you speak of anything
Be sure you know it's true.

I've put a seal upon my lips
To help me guard with care
The thing I say with swift repeat;
O tongue of mine beware.
(Nothing is opened by mistake more than the human mouth.)

Tim and I talked over our problems, got things straightened out.
I'm trying to help everyone.
Because we are Christians, we live for God.
God said love one another.
When we have problems, there's only one way we can love each other.

Since the Lord your debt did pay.
Saved your soul in grace one day.
You with charity should live.
Always ready to forgive.

(The best way to kill an enemy is to make him your friend.)
Forgiveness is the only way we can love one another.

"That Saturday night, we studied the gifts that God has given to people and the fact that every believer *does* have a spiritual gift," Miller says. "We looked into the Bible to find out what the gifts are and how a person can determine which ones he or she has. Then we put on Billy Preston's album called *Behold.* Preston used to be very big in secular music, but now he plays Christian rock. We played both sides of the record that night and sang along with him."

There was no way for anyone to know how significant the last two lines of one of their favorite songs on that album would soon be. Here are the words to that song:

I'm giving my life to Christ
For Him to do as He chooses.
I'm putting my trust in Him
He's a God that never loses.

For Him I'd sacrifice
everything
He's not pleased with.
On Calvary
He paid the price
So I may have eternal life—Hallelujah!

Give God some of our time
So He can lead us
and guide us.
We must let His light shine.
Let me know that He's precious.
There'll be no toil or strife
He makes things calm and easy.
Yes, He does.

On Calvary He paid the price
So we may have eternal life.

8

Going Home

Shortly after nine o'clock, the final verse of the last song had been sung. Now it was time to wrap up the evening by chowing down a little, snacks not being a part of the Bible-study time the way they were at Salt and Light. Usually, the group went to Friendly's restaurant. This night, though, some voices were raised in favor of going around the corner from Randy's place to Lisa's Pizza and bringing soda and pizza back to the apartment. Friendly's? Lisa's? When agreement was reached, everyone piled into three vehicles—Brian's van and cars driven by Randy and Betty—and took off for Friendly's a couple miles north in Hillsdale.

Those who did not slide into booths sat at the first U-shaped counter, which was part of the decor before this Friendly's was remodeled. There was less hesitancy about what to order than there had been about where to go. Maria and Beth went for hot fudge sundaes, as always. Eric had a hot dog, coffee and a glass of ice. Part of his routine was to put ice cubes in his coffee cup, which he had the waitress refill three or four times that night. Most of the other boys gobbled up hamburgers and French fries, which they washed down with Fribbles, Friendly's super-thick milk shakes. Between bites and sips, Mark rendered his inimitable chipmunk rendition, drawing chuckles with his squeaky-voiced monologue.

Maria almost always rode home with Betty, who lived only about three miles from her, and it had been her intention to do so that evening. But Maria's plans changed. That's why Maria, who was seated a few chairs from Betty at the counter, passed her a note she had written on—of all things—the back of the report card Brian had received that day. Her note, which she had scrawled while at Miller's apartment and which she forgot to pass along until this moment, read:

Betty,
I'm going to Friendly's with the Hayhursts. I have a ride home with
them. Thanks anyway.

Maria

Maria knew she had to do one other thing: call her mother to let her
know that she would probably be a little late getting home. That night,
Maria was particularly thankful to be with her friends, knowing she
had come *so* close to missing the meeting because she had accepted a
babysitting assignment for that same evening. After Maria found out
that there was to be a Bible study on November 11th, she was in a
quandary: She wanted to be with her friends, but she had promised to
sit with Michael, the infant child of a couple who lived close to her, Dr.
and Mrs. Mark Doctor. Once she had made up her mind that she preferred going to the study, Maria asked her father if she could have his
permission to get out of her job for that Saturday. Never before would
Walter Van Beers have consented to do such a thing. This time,
though, he felt Maria had done so much babysitting and had been so
good in other ways, that she had earned the right to join her friends.
Besides, it wasn't as if she was skipping out on work to go carousing;
she was going to a Bible study. It was 10:15 when Maria called her
mother from Friendly's.

At the same time, Johnny Hartman and his family drove into
Westwood. Johnny was a regular at the youth meetings but had not
been able to attend Saturday's study because he and his family had
gone to a birthday party, his grandmother's eighty-second.

"As we drove through town, I looked to see if there were any lights
on in Randy's apartment," Johnny recalled. "No lights were on. 'Just
like them to go to Friendly's,' I said. My dad said, 'Do you want to go
there?' I told him, 'Yes.' Then I remembered the Rangers' game was
on TV. I hadn't seen the Rangers in awhile and I wanted to watch the
game. So I changed my mind about going to Friendly's."

While Johnny watched the Rangers defeat the Pittsburgh Penguins
2-1, his companions spilled out of Friendly's and into the parking lot.
It was time for those who had not already decided on how to get home
to settle that matter, one that wasn't all that important. Or was it?

Henry Van Der Werf, who was going to go with Brian, changed his
mind in the parking lot. "I lived almost around the corner," he says. "I
figured I wanted to get home and that by the time Brian dropped off
everyone he had it would be quite awhile. It was a sudden decision on

my part not to go with Brian." And so it was that Henry climbed in Betty's car.

Tommy, Maria, Beth, and Mark were already in the van with Brian. "You're going to come home with me, aren't you?" Brian called to Timmy. Timmy wanted to go with Brian. "The week before, though, I'd had a run-in with my parents because I got home late," Timmy says. "I went over to the van. I wanted to go with Brian, but I was supposed to be home by 11. My parents didn't like me riding to Upper Saddle River to take the girls home first. I struggled with the situation. If I was late, I *knew* I'd get yelled at. Randy and I were close friends, so I went home with him." And so it was that Timmy went in the Firebird with Randy.

Rob also wanted to go in the van, but his sister Betty nixed that notion because it was getting late, a little past 10:30. "I *pleaded* with my sister to let me go," Rob points out. "I just wanted to go for the ride. Brian and I were *very* close friends and we both enjoyed cars. When my sister wouldn't let me go, I was infuriated." And so it was that Rob got into the car with his sister.

Somewhere amid the sounds of engines and voices, Brian or Mark called out, "Hey Eric, you wanna come with us?"

"Eric was already in my car," Betty remembers. "He hesitated for only an instant and then he got out and went in the van." In his own quiet, self-controlled way, Eric likely felt a touch of the special kind of joy one savors when longed-for pals make an effort to build a friendship. Sure it was out of the way for Eric and Tommy—to be going with the Hayhurst brothers, who would have to head north to drop off Beth and Maria before coming back south to Westwood. Camaraderie is not to be underestimated, however. Many were the nights when members of the youth group drove around longer than they had to for one reason: the pleasure of being in each other's company. And so it was that Eric got in the van.

Mark stretched out his long and lanky frame as he sat in the seat up front next to Brian, who fiddled with the dial on the radio and pulled out of the parking lot. Tommy sat next to the window in the back seat. Beside him was Eric. The girls chose to kneel on the floor of the van— Beth behind Brian and Maria behind Mark. One of the boys in the front turned up the volume of the radio. As Brian drove toward Beth's house, the teens sang along with the songs that were being played on the radio. After ten or so rollicking minutes, they arrived at Beth's house. When Beth noticed that her parents had not come home yet, she said, "We can keep going." Thus, Brian drove off so that they could all keep rolling along for a few more minutes. A song by the Beatles—"Revolution 1"—blared forth from the radio. While Brian drove slowly around the streets of Allendale, the teens sang along with the Beatles: "You say you want a revolution/Well you know we all want to change the world/. . . You say you got a real solution/Well you know we'd all love to see the plan." Their voices were a little more emphatic when it came time to singing the chorus: "Don't you know it's gonna be alright. Alright, Alright." The next time Brian drove up to Beth's house, she saw that her folks were home so she said goodbye to the five and got out of the van.

Now it was time for Brian to drive freckle-faced Maria home. Mark ran his fingers through his blond hair. Tommy peered through his glasses into the darkness of the night. Eric soaked up the pleasure of being part of this scene. Brian drove East along Allendale Avenue until he reached East Saddle River Road in Saddle River. There he turned left. Another couple miles and he would have Maria at her house in Upper Saddle River.

East Saddle River Road is narrow and unlit by overhead lights. For years, residents along this stretch of road had complained that lights were needed because the road is shoulderless and has twists in it that are not the easiest to negotiate. Brian drove a mile north, passed Albert Drive and was on a relatively straight section of the road in Upper Saddle River. Up ahead, he spotted lights coming toward him, lights he had a hard time seeing because the oncoming vehicles were partially hidden as they entered a dip in the road. Brian, with his fine reflexes, must have sensed at once that there was something unusual about those lights. There was: There were *two* sets of lights speeding toward him and one set of lights was in *his* lane. There was no where to turn.

Don't you know it's gonna be alright. Alright, Alright.
On Calvary He paid the price
So we may have eternal life.

Can you hear them?

9

Waiting and Searching

Headlights. They were coming at Brian in his lane because the driver of the onrushing van was passing a car. John McNally, the nineteen-year-old driver of the car being passed, pulled off to the extreme right of the southbound lane when he saw the two vans collide. The horror of what McNally and three teenagers riding with him saw horrified them all. Two of those youths ran to a nearby house and knocked on the door. Mark Tollette, 18, answered, listened while the boys told him there had been a terrible accident, and then phoned the Upper Saddle River police. It was 11:07 P.M.

"I was loading my gear—flashlight, nightstick, and stuff—into a vehicle when the night clerk told me there had been an accident," Patrolman Gary Ahlers says. "I went from headquarters to the scene on East Saddle River Road. I was the first police officer at the scene. I wasn't new to accidents. I had been a captain with the Upper Saddle River rescue squad before joining the police and we had dealt mainly with the extrication of victims. When I got to the scene, it was strange to me. Usually when there's a serious accident, you hear crying or moaning or maybe gurgling from the victims. The only sound I heard when I got out of the car that night and ran to the vehicles that had crashed was the water coming out of the radiator of the Stricklett van. It was hissing. There were no signs of life anywhere.

"I went back to the car to advise the desk what vehicles were needed. Then I checked the victims for vital signs. There were none. [By 11:20, an ambulance and vehicles from the fire department and rescue squad had arrived.] At first, we counted only five victims. Then we found one more boy [Mark] under the Hayhurst van and another victim under the other van."

Those in the other vehicle were brothers, Roger and Stuart Stricklett. Roger, 28, was the driver of the 1973 Ford Econoline van. Stuart, 26, was a college graduate who had a job in the mailroom of a publishing company and lived with his parents in Allendale. That was where the brothers were going at the time of the accident. Roger, who was married, was in the roofing and home-improvement business.

Waiting. Where is he? Why doesn't he call? Where could they have gone? Who would know? Is there *anybody* I can call? Waiting's partner in time is worry. And worry is the bullet created by the mind. Worry pierces the heart with doubt, concern, torment. Nothing else creates the same sense of awfulness. Waiting. Maybe they had car trouble? Time stretches. An agonizing hour turns out to have been only minutes. Alternate moments of terrifying fear ("Is he being operated on in some hospital now?") and of hope ("He's been late before and always made it home all right"). Waiting. The questions rush through the mind. Answers—they were the only remedy. When there are no answers, the bullet pierces more deeply. Waiting. It turns the mind into a canvas. Pictures are painted. Not Rembrandts, though. Waiting. It drains. Hours struggle past. Maybe a cup of coffee will help. What could have happened? Something *must* have happened. Probably nothing too serious. But I've got to know. Waiting. Sometimes the vigil *is* rewarded: A loved one arrives, explains, not possibly being able to appreciate why the waiting one's sigh seems to come from the toes. Sometimes the vigil is *not* rewarded.

"It's eleven thirty and Eric's not home yet," Mary Jane Borloz said to her husband Howard. "I think we should call to find out what's wrong. Eric always calls when he knows he's going to be late."

"Wait till twelve," Howard suggested.

Barbara Hayhurst was also getting edgy while she waited downstairs for her sons. It was nearing midnight when she went upstairs and woke up her husband Don to let him know that Mark and Brian were not yet home.

Next door, Martha Carroll was the one keeping a watchful eye and a listening ear. Each time she heard the sound of a vehicle that seemed to be a van, she allowed herself to feel a little relief. But each time Martha got up from her spot on the far end of the living room couch to look outside, and did not see Tommy hurrying up the driveway, she sagged inwardly.

Walt and Connie Van Beers were asleep. After receiving the call from Maria, Connie had gone to bed and tried to stay awake to listen for Maria's arrival. Even if she didn't hear Maria come in, Connie knew that her daughter would wake her up to let her know that she had made it home safely.

Jim Robertson, Beth's father, was driving his son Jim and his girl-friend Sue to her house, which was near where the Van Beerses lived. A minute or so after turning off Allendale Avenue onto East Saddle River Road, they found that the road had been blocked off. As a result, they took a slightly more circuitous route to Upper Saddle River. On the way back home, Jim and his son came south on East Saddle River. When they got to Elmer's, a gas station and grocery store at the first main intersection, they saw that there was a roadblock there, too. Jim Robertson, never one to gawk at accidents, felt a strange compulsion ("It was like something *made* me go there") to find out more about the crash that had obviously taken place. After maneuvering his car around a few back streets, he came down a hill toward the site of the accident. He and his son walked the last hundred yards until, in the glow of bright spotlights that had been set up, they could see that two vans had collided. There they saw a body lying in a shallow ditch just off the edge of the road. They also saw the sheet-covered body of a girl. That much they were sure of because all that was left uncovered was her long hair. Auburn hair.

Martha Carroll mentioned her concern to her son Bill, who had just come in from working on carpeting the interior of the family van. Bill was hunting through the refrigerator when his mother mentioned that she was thinking of calling Randy Miller to find out if he knew where Tommy was or why he was so late. "Don't pester him now," was Bill's advice. "Tommy'll be home soon." After a few more minutes, at the point where she "couldn't stand it any more," Martha phoned Miller at 12 o'clock. Randy said he didn't know where Tommy was, but he tried to comfort Martha by saying, "I'm *sure* everything's all right." Least comforted at all by those words was Randy himself. While he tossed around in bed, Randy thought, "There's probably been an acci-dent." Then, as pictures of what might have happened raced through his mind, he said aloud, "No. No."

A few minutes after midnight, Howard Borloz agreed with his wife that there was some cause for concern. Howard got in his van and five minutes later was in front of the Hayhurst house. What he was looking for was the Hayhurst van. It was not there. As much as he might have wanted to go into the house to ask Barbara or Don if they had any idea what was wrong, Howard did not want to impose. So he drove back home. He hoped that by the time he arrived Eric would be home, or Mary Jane would have some information. Neither was the case.

It was 12:30 when Donna Van Beers let herself into her house after returning from babysitting at a neighbor's. Dutifully, she went into her parents' bedroom and shook her mother until it registered with Connie that Donna was home.

Although groggy, Connie said, "Check Maria's room and see if she's home." Donna went downstairs, looked, returned to her mother's bedside and said, "She's not there." Connie looked at her alarm clock. Realizing that Maria should have been home more than an hour earlier, she jostled Walt out of his sleep. When Connie said it was 12:30 and Maria wasn't home yet, Walt responded: "You always worry. Relax." As soon as his drowsiness wore off, though, Walt was out of bed. Meanwhile, Connie was making phone calls.

By now, Howard Borloz was back in his van and headed toward the Hayhursts once again, looking all the while for the van that would be bringing his son home. At the Hayhursts, Don and Barbara and Howard tried to assure each other that their sons' delay had probably been caused by nothing more than a flat tire. Or mechanical failure. Or an empty gas tank. You know how kids are: They laugh so much that they forget to keep an eye on the gas needle.

Beth Robertson had fallen asleep in front of the television set at home. When her father and brother returned, she woke up. "We came across a terrible accident on East Saddle River Road," Beth's dad said rather solemnly. "Two vans."

Hearing about an accident was nothing new, but when Beth heard the word "vans" it was almost as if she had been jabbed with a pin. "What kind of vans?" she asked with deliberate casualness. When she didn't get a quick reply, Beth added the question that was most on her mind: "Was one a VW?"

"I think so," her father replied.

The first call that Connie Van Beers made was to Beth Robertson, who she knew would have been dropped off at home just before Brian would have brought Maria home.

"Beth, do you know where Maria is?" Connie inquired.

"No."

"What time did you get home?"

"Uh, eleven thirty," Beth fibbed, hoping that by adding half an hour to her arrival time Connie might not be quite so worried.

"That was an hour ago. Where is Maria?"

"I'm not sure what way they went home," Beth replied. "Maybe she went over to the Hayhursts with Brian and Mark."

"Is something wrong, Beth?" asked Connie, who felt she detected something in the tone of the girl's voice.

"All I can tell you is that my father was taking Jim's girlfriend home to Upper Saddle River and he saw an accident on East Saddle River Road."

Nothing made much sense to Connie. There were too many gaps. Too little reliable information. She phoned the Hayhursts and asked if Brian and Mark were home yet. Barbara said they weren't but that her husband was just getting ready to go with Howard Borloz to see if they could find the van and give whatever help was needed. It all sounded highly logical. Before the call was over, a search plan was agreed upon so that Howard and Don would not go over the same territory that the Van Beerses would be covering.

Connie made a third call. It was to the Upper Saddle River police. "I hear there's been an accident on East Saddle River Road," she began. "Can you tell me if a red Volkswagen van was involved?" This might have been the most important phone call of her life, but all Connie Van Beers received for an answer was a predictably flat and entirely correct-according-to-the-rules reply, "We can't give out any information yet." As uninformative as that response was, it somehow triggered a nervous reaction in Connie. All of a sudden, she was possessed by a feeling of urgency. Now she had substantiated the fact that there had been an accident not far from her house and that it was on the road that Maria would have been traveling.

"Walter, let's go," she half-yelled.

"Take it easy," Walt replied.

"Let's go," Connie said again. Then she told Donna, "We're going out looking to see what we can find out."

Martha Carroll waited until 1:30 before she awakened her husband Larry. Together, they prayed. "Will you call the Hayhursts?" said Martha, desperate for any shred of news. "I don't feel calm any more and I don't think I could talk on the phone." Larry agreed to call. Because he was ill and was having trouble with his coordination, Martha dialed the number and then handed the receiver to her husband.

"Howard and Don are going to drive around to find the kids," Barbara told Larry. "The Van Beerses are going out, too. Don's going to call me when he gets to Upper Saddle River and I'll call you back."

At 1:30, the desk officer at the Westwood police headquarters received a call from the Upper Saddle River police explaining that there had been a bad accident, that one of the vehicles might be from Westwood and that help was needed with identifying some of the victims. He notified Detective John Graef, who was on duty, of the call. Nothing struck Graef until he heard that "One of the vans is reddish with white trim." Immediately, a name popped into Graef's mind: *The Hayhursts*. He knew the family well. Yes, Graef said, he'd go to Upper Saddle River to try to help with identification.

Shortly before 2 A.M., Donna Van Beers, *convinced* that something was terribly wrong, phoned Beth Robertson. "What's happened? What's happened?" Donna wanted to know.

"I'll be right over," Beth said. She then told her father about Donna's call, got into the car with him, and took off for the Van Beerses' house.

Patrolman Ahlers, as part of his routine when checking out an accident, looked at the speedometers in both vehicles. These readings, he knew from past experiences, were "usually accurate to within a few miles an hour." When he glanced at the speedometer in the Hayhurst van he noted that it had stopped "just at thirty-five miles an hour." A check of the speedometer in the Stricklett van showed that it was "over one hundred miles an hour."

Don Hayhurst and Howard Borloz, who was driving, began their search by traveling north through Westwood, Hillsdale, and Woodcliff Lake. No sign of the van.

Connie filled Walt in on the calls she had made, on the information she had picked up, and on the questions and fears that were pulling at her. It didn't take long for Walt to grasp the magnitude of what his wife was saying and why she was so anxious. Now, for the first time, Walt could feel fear pushing up inside him. It was only a two-minute drive down the road before they came to the traffic light at Elmer's. As Walt got closer, both he and Connie could pick out a police car, a rescue ambulance, and a barricade. Walt pulled off to the right and into the parking lot next to Elmer's. Then the Van Beerses got out and walked toward the roadblock. The lights. The people. The vehicles that were there. The barricade. Connie's mind put the scraps of information together with what she had found out earlier. As she got near the barricade, Connie called out, "Maria. Where is she? *Where is she?*" A policeman who knew Connie came up to her and stood in her path as she tried to walk onto the road.

"You can't go down there," he told Connie.

"Maria!"

"You can't go down there," the policeman repeated.

"Maria!"

10

The Longest Night

Connie was frantic. She tried to elude the policeman, but he clutched her by the arms and, in answer to Connie's half question-half plea, said: "She's gone." *Instantly,* Connie collapsed. Walt grabbed her before she crumpled to the pavement.

"This is odd," was the first thought in Walt's mind. "I've always been an optimistic person. I can't believe this is happening to me."

Walt Van Beers quickly knew that it was, indeed, happening to him. He and Connie were both put in the rescue squad ambulance because it was obvious neither was in any shape to drive home.

"God, why did you do this?" Walt said in the ambulance that was taking Connie and him to their house. "How could you let this happen? We've been trying so hard to be what you want us to be. We've given our lives to you. God, *how could you do this?*"

As soon as the ambulance pulled into the Van Beerses' driveway, Donna came to the front door. Then, seeing her father get out of the ambulance, Donna ran outside and loudly asked, "What's happened? Where's Maria?"

"She's gone," her father told her. "She's gone."

At that instant, Jim and Beth Robertson drove up to the house. They saw the ambulance.

"I don't believe it," Donna shouted after hearing her father's words. "I don't believe it. I don't believe it."

It was with the force of a thunderbolt, or so it seemed, that Jim Robertson was startled by a realization: The girl lying on the road with the sheet over her had been Maria. He felt the wisest move would be to go to Randy Miller's, tell him what he had seen and what Beth knew about who was in the van. *Something* had to be done.

No sooner had the Robertsons driven off than Don Hayhurst and Howard Borloz arrived. They saw the ambulance attendants coming out the front door. "Uh oh, what's happened?" Howard said. Thinking that they might get some details from the attendants, Howard and Don asked them what was going on. The ambulance crew told them there had been an accident, which one described as "the worst I've ever seen." They added that Maria was dead and that "others" had died in the crash. From there on, no matter how the fathers pressed for details, no matter how much they stressed that they had sons who were involved in the accident, the attendants refused to say more. ("Souls of discretion," Howard thought to himself. "God bless 'em.")

When Don and Howard went into the house, they saw that Connie, who was seated on a living room couch, was staring blankly and that she was unaware of what was going on around her. Walt shook his head and, with more and more anger, kept asking. *"God, why did you do this?"* Howard and Don were both slightly stunned. Even while expressing their sympathy to the Van Beerses, they began to fathom that if it was true that "others" had been killed, their sons might be dead.

Both men then remembered that they had promised to call home. Howard phoned Mary Jane from the kitchen and gave her the news. Don called Barbara, who phoned Larry Carroll with the word that Maria was dead and that others had been killed. "Remember, Larry, those are *our* kids who were in that van," Barbara said. Larry's response: "Yes, Barbara. We've got to throw ourselves on the mercy of the Lord." After hanging up the phone, Larry said out loud, "Father, we commit this night into your care so that we will be able to live by the facts and not according to our emotions." Larry, an intensely spiritual man, was attempting to gird himself for the worst.

At the Van Beerses', Connie passed out and slumped down on the couch. A female member of the ambulance squad that had come to the house quickly administered oxygen from a small tank. After Connie came around, Walt knelt next to his wife and held her hands.

It seemed that hearing the two men use the phone gave Walt an idea. Into the kitchen he went. Quickly, he dialed one of the men who had been instrumental in his recent development as a Christian— Pierre Biscaye. While Pierre slept on, his wife Nedaleine reached across him for the receiver. Walt Van Beers, normally a gentleman in all respects, didn't care who he was talking to; he just had to unload. Which is exactly what he did. "Why would God allow Maria to die?" Walt wanted to know. "Where is this God you've been telling me such great things about?"

* * *

Pastor Fred Beveridge

Within minutes, Pierre was dressed and on his way. "Might need my Bible," he thought as he grabbed it from the nightstand beside his bed. Then he was on his way to Pascack Valley Hospital in Westwood. Once he got there, Pierre went to the emergency ward, which is where he was sure the Van Beerses would be. They were not and no one there knew about Maria being dead or about any major accident. A call to Nedaleine clarified things for Pierre: Walt was at home.

By now, quite a few phones were buzzing. Just how busy the telephone wires were was something Barbara found out when she called the Beveridges, McCarthys, and Biscayes. All those families had already been informed about the accident. One reason the phones were so busy was because, even back then, there was a uniqueness to the congregation of the Pascack Bible Church. It wasn't just that the members referred to themselves more often as "the body" rather than as "the church." (That is an allusion to the fact that the church is considered to be the physical representation of Christ—the "body of Christ"—until He returns again.) What those members called themselves was secondary to how they put feet to their faith. This they did in many ways, one of which was to share the needs and burdens of fellow members. A program that included "undershepherds" and "Care-Rings" went a long way toward drawing the parishioners closer and closer together in a spirit of Christian love and unity. That's why Nedaleine Biscaye phoned the McCarthys and the Cussimanios. Tom and Flo Cussimanio, close friends of the Van Beerses, left for Upper Saddle River within minutes after being told of the crash.

Howard Borloz was also on the phone. "I know that there is certain information you cannot release yet," he said when he got through to the Upper Saddle River police office. "But you must understand that we are talking about my son's life. I would appreciate any information you can give me about my son or any of the others in the accident."

Larry and Martha Carroll would like to have gone to be with the others at the Van Beerses' residence, but the seats in the Carrolls' van had been taken out for the carpeting project and they had not yet been replaced. Mary Jane Borloz stayed home because she felt a call might come from a hospital, a call that would give her some clue about the condition of Eric.

"It didn't happen," Connie Van Beers said as she sat almost transfixed in the living room. "She's coming home. She's coming home."
"No," Walt said. "She's gone. Maria's gone."

A ringing of his doorbell caused Randy Miller to hold his breath for a few seconds while he waited to make certain he had heard correctly. He had. There was a second ring. Miller, who had not fallen asleep, got up, slipped into a pair of trousers and opened the door. There stood Beth Robertson and her father.
"Maria's dead," Beth said, as tears rivered down her cheeks.
"Nah," was the first thing that Randy could utter. "She's all right. Don't worry about her."
"No, Randy," Jim Robertson said. "Maria is dead."
"Come in," Miller said.
What sketchy details the Robertsons had, they passed along to Randy, who groped for the right words to say. Randy, noticing that Beth was still sobbing, felt he had found a comforting thought. "They're with the Lord."

Beth looked up. There was a slight smile on Randy's face. This enraged Beth, who shouted, "Don't tell me that." Miller's theology may have been correct, but all Beth cared about at that time was that she had lost her dearest friend.

Taken aback, Miller thought: *What do I do, Lord?* He knew he had to call Pastor Beveridge. When his phone jangled, Fred Beveridge got out of bed and made his way across the bedroom, flicked on a light and grabbed the phone on his wife's dresser. By that time, his mind was developing half-thoughts that it was a call from his brother and his sister-in-law. Pastor Beveridge had been worried that Don and Gale might have stayed at his house later than they should have that evening before beginning their drive back to Atlantic City. Then he heard Randy's voice. "There's been an accident and Maria Van Beers has been killed," Randy began. "Are you sure?" inquired Pastor Beveridge, who was shocked into being awake. Said Randy: "I think so. Beth Robertson and her father are here and they say that the Hayhurst van was in an accident and they think some more of the kids might have been killed."

"Who else was in the van?" Pastor inquired.

"I'm not sure. Brian and Mark. Tommy Carroll. Henry Van Der Werf, I think. I'm just not sure."

"Do any of the parents know?"

"The Van Beerses do. I don't know who else."

"Are the Robertsons still there?"

"Yes," Randy said. "Fred, I need your help. I need it like *I've never needed it before.*"

"I'll be right over."

Detective Graef arrived at the scene of the crash at 2:30. Maria, he was told, was the girl covered with a sheet. Graef could not bring himself to look at her, for he knew her well, knew Walt and Connie, and had socialized with the family.

Ten minutes after hanging up the phone, Pastor Beveridge was in Miller's apartment. He, Randy, and the Robertsons prayed. A call was placed to the Reverend Bill Wortman, the church's Minister of Discipleship, asking him to come to the apartment. Barbara Hayhurst called Randy and was promised a ride up to the Van Beerses'.

Then the Robertsons departed in their car, and Miller and Reverend

Wortman climbed into the back seat of Pastor's '77 Chevy wagon, leaving room on the front seat for Barbara.

"I *know* Brian is dead," Barbara said. "He was driving. Maria's dead and so are others, so he must be."

"We have to pray that everyone will have strength and that Satan won't get one ounce of benefit from whatever takes place," Wortman suggested. Pray they did. Out loud. With fervor, with hope.

A few minutes behind Pastor's car was Bob McCarthy, who had waited at the Hayhurst house until Ben Nelson arrived. Ben was the fiance of the Hayhursts' daughter—blonde, demure Corinne. When he arrived, all three got into McCarthy's car and drove off. In an effort to dispell the uneasiness that they all felt, Bob sang Christian songs. The words gave *him* encouragement and Bob could only hope that Ben and Corinne felt as uplifted.

"My son was in one of the vans," Howard Borloz was saying as he got through to the police department again. "His mother's anxiously waiting at home. Can't you give me *any* news?"

By now, the Cussimanios had arrived and Pierre Biscaye had made the long trip from the hospital to the Van Beerses. Pierre, who still had only the flimsiest idea of what had happened, hurriedly opened the front door of the house and, as he entered, brushed past Howard Borloz. *Why's he here?* was a thought that sped through Pierre's mind. His uppermost thought, however, was about Walt and Connie. Walt was seated on a sofa while Don Hayhurst tried to console him. When Pierre came over, Walt looked up and, in a loud voice, asked: "Why did God do this? Why would God take Maria? Why would He allow this? Can you tell me?"

"Why are all these people here?" asked Connie in a limp monotone. She had no idea that word of the accident was spreading or that other members of the youth group might have been killed. It was 2:45 in the morning. In the past few minutes, cars driven by Jim Robertson, Pastor Beveridge, and Bob McCarthy had arrived. When Barbara Hayhurst entered the house, she and Don embraced, closed their eyes and held on for a few seconds. There were no words. What could they say?

Altogether, there were now seventeen people downstairs: the Van Beerses (Connie, Walt and Donna), the Robertsons (Beth and Jim), the Cussimanios (Tom and Flo), the Hayhursts (Don, Barbara and Corinne), Howard Borloz, Reverend Wortman, Randy Miller, Pierre

Biscaye, Bob McCarthy, Ben Nelson, and Pastor Beveridge. Five-year-old John Van Beers was asleep upstairs. Martha and Larry Carroll waited and prayed at home. They called their son Larry Jr., who came over to be with them. They also phoned their son Alan in Virginia and asked him to pray. Bill prayed, too. Mary Jane Borloz waited alone until 3 A.M. when her son Andy, seeing lights on in the house when he woke up, joined her in the living room.

Many of the adults at Walt and Connie's house began drifting from room to room—to the kitchen, to the dining room, to the family room that was to the left of the living room. Some sipped coffee that Flo had made. Tears were dabbed. Pierre read to Walt from the Psalms: "I waited patiently for the Lord, and he inclined unto me, and heard my cry. . . . Blessed is that man that maketh the Lord his trust. . . ."

Howard, who had phoned the police department a number of times and then called his wife after each effort to say that there was no news, called again. *"You must understand, my son was in that accident,"* he said. "His mother is at home waiting to find out if he's dead or alive. *All of us* want to know about our children. Can't you give us *any* information?"

Don went to Walt to comfort him with verses of Scripture. Moments later, caught up in fears that he could no longer suppress, Don sat on the steps leading to the second floor, closed his eyes, put his head down, and prayed. Howard went outside to walk around.

Inside, more and more people did more and more drifting. Some banded together to pray. When Beth noticed that Barbara went to some people to offer comfort or hope, she was impressed by the realization that, "She's helping others and she doesn't even know if her sons are dead or alive." That, plus the knowledge of what her father had told her about the accident, caused Beth to break down in tears. Jim Robertson wept, too. Seeing this, Barbara tried to console both of them. "The Lord is my shepherd," Pierre began as he sought to comfort Don. Minutes afterward, Don attempted to soothe Walt, who was weeping. "Why are all these people here?" Connie wondered aloud again. Most of the men gathered in the dining room, formed a circle, and wrapped their arms around one another's shoulders. There they stood for five minutes or more as they wept and prayed. Don Hayhurst called the police. He was told, "Our information is now a little more complete," and "We'll send an officer to give you some details."

Waiting for so long without getting any information added to everyone's anxiety. That's why four men—Pastor Beveridge, Howard, Bob, and Pierre—decided they had to do something. They went to get answers. At Elmer's, though, they were told there was no one there who could provide them with any details. Detective Graef, a member of the Pascack Bible Church, was only able to tell them that he didn't know the youngsters well enough to make positive identifications. When he added that a priest was at the crash site, Howard raised his voice. "They don't need a priest down there," he said, knowing the clergyman had been summoned to give the last rites to the victim or victims. It was Howard's way of lashing out at the prospect that his son might have been in such need. Their efforts frustrated, the men left.

After the four had paced around the Van Beerses' lawn for awhile, Howard said, "This is ridiculous. People have been waiting for hours to know if their sons are alive and they keep telling us to wait some more." If nothing else, the four men had found out on their trip to the barricade that the process of making identifications had not been completed. Knowing that everyone—not just Howard—was frazzled, Pastor Beveridge said, "I'm going back and tell them I'm the kids' pastor and that I can help with the identifications. Anybody want to come with me?" Pierre agreed to go along. Off they went in Pastor Beveridge's station wagon. Bob McCarthy followed in his car, intending to wait at the roadblock if the other two were allowed to go beyond there.

Meanwhile, Flo was becoming concerned that Connie, whose eyes were still glazed, might need medical attention. So Flo phoned Dr. Ronald Allen, Connie's physician. Her call was taken by an answering service. A few minutes later, Dr. Allen called and suggested that Connie be put to bed. Several of the men lifted Connie from the couch, carried her upstairs, and put her on her bed. Before going upstairs to be with his wife, Walt stood at the foot of the steps, held onto the banister and said, "Oh God, I don't understand, but I'm gonna try not to be bitter."

At the roadblock, Pastor Beveridge was stopped by a policeman. He identified himself and explained who Pierre was. Using a walkie-talkie, the officer contacted a superior at the accident scene and, receiving the go-ahead, allowed Pastor to drive on. When he saw that many other cars and emergency vehicles were up ahead, Pastor Beveridge pulled his station wagon over to the side of the road. Then he and Pierre began their walk into a form of reality that seemed unreal. It was 3:50 A.M.

Although both wore jackets and although the temperature was a little above 50, the two men could feel their entire bodies—even, it seemed, their very beings—shivering. To themselves, they prayed for God's strength for what lay ahead. The first warning they had that their senses would be assaulted as never before came when they saw that the area ahead of them was aglow with light. Three spotlights, which seemed to both men to be mounted in trees that lined the road, were perched atop extension poles attached to the side of a rescue squad vehicle. The beams from these halogen lights, and from six that had been placed at ground level, were so intense that the site was daylight-bright. But the faint bluish tinge to their glow made the scene appear other-worldly. The engines and generators of emergency vehicles whirred and—blended together—filled the otherwise silent night with a heavy hum. Thoughts lodged in the men's minds:

Pierre: *It's eerie. We're walking out of total darkness into total brightness.*

Pastor Beveridge: *It's eerie. I'm so nervous that I'm vibrating. God, please be with us. Give us strength."*

A police officer walked up to the two men, explained that three victims had not yet been identified and wanted to know if Pastor Bevveridge and Pierre would help with the process. They said they would.

"I've got to warn you, what you're going to see is going to be *extremely* unpleasant," the officer pointed out. "Are you sure you're willing to do this?" Both men, perhaps because they were now speechless, nodded their consent.

On they walked. Both had the same thought as they got closer: *It's like a battleground.* Emergency vehicles—police cars, rescue trucks, ambulances, fire engines—lined both sides of the road. Some thirty people from these vehicles stood in small clusters or paced around with their hands jammed in their jacket pockets. Here, as back at the Van Beerses' house, there had been much waiting.

A few steps farther and the two men were engulfed in another dimension of their ordeal. There, covered except for her auburn hair and a booted foot, lay Maria, face down. She was near the right rear wheel of the Hayhurst van, which was upright. Less than ten feet away was Eric. He and Maria were the only two in the Hayhurst van who had been identified so far. The van, which had been going north at the time of the accident, was now facing south, having been swung completely around by the impact of the crash. From the driver's seat to the rear seat, the left side of the van had been torn off. Most of the other side was gone, too, having given way under the impact of three of the youngsters who had been hurtled against it. The other van, which had been headed south, was lying on the passenger side and was pointing north. Both vans were in the northbound lane, the Hayhurst vehicle slightly diagonal and with its front bumper aimed toward the double yellow line that ran down the center of the blacktop road. (Trying to piece together details, it appeared that Brian had veered to the right to avoid the oncoming van and that the other driver tried to cut to *his* right to get back into the lane where he belonged. When the vans hit, they were both angled and apparently tore into each other with such force that they were interlocked briefly and spun each other around.)

Whatever glimmer of hope the two men might have held onto that any of the four boys in that van might somehow have survived was eradicated when they looked at the vehicle. Brian, Mark, and Tommy had not yet been identified by anyone because all their personal effects had been scattered over a wide area.

Pierre and Pastor Beveridge went about their task separately, silently. They spoke only when they were able to tell the police officer that they could give positive identification. Having seen Maria and Eric lying on the road, the men presumed that they would find the others there also. They didn't. Inside the van, near the centerpost on the passenger side, was one of the boys. "That's Tommy Carroll," Pastor Beveridge told the officer. Another youngster was found closer to the front, but it was hard to tell which one it was. "Dear Lord, please help me through this," Pastor Beveridge prayed. He went on. There was a moment, he would later say, when: "I felt I was being pushed to my emotional limits by my adrenalin."

Off to the left of the van and five feet behind where it had come to a rest, the men saw a crumpled form lying just off the edge of the road in a shallow spillway. It was Brian. By the process of elimination, it meant that the boy under the van who had not yet been identified must be Mark. After another look, it was determined that, yes, it was Mark. Five large green baggage-type tags were filled out by the police with the names of the five youngsters. They were attached to the bodies by means of wires on the tags.

Less than half an hour after they had come to the site, Pastor Beveridge and Pierre left, each placing an arm around the other's back as they walked to the station wagon. Nervous chills. The men now realized that the chills had gone away while they were busy with their job of making identifications. Now, however, they were back. Before them was yet another painful task: The parents back at the house had to be told that their sons were dead. As he drove past the barricade, Pastor Beveridge did not stop to say anything to Bob. He didn't have to; Bob could read their solemn faces.

Howard was pacing around on the lawn when the two cars pulled up in the road below. As tenderly as he could, Pastor Beveridge told him that Eric and the other three boys were all dead. Howard stood motionless. "I can't believe it," he said. Bob, who felt a closeness with him because of his recent dealings with Eric, remained outside with Howard while the other two men went inside.

When the people who were waiting inside had heard the cars arrive, they gathered in the living room. Knowing that it was his responsibility to be the spokesman, Pastor Beveridge walked to the center of the room and broke the news: "They're all gone. All the kids are with the Lord."

Silence. Minds tried to grasp the just-spoken words. Then a few heavy sighs. A few heads bowed as tears came. Pastor Beveridge turned to Barbara Hayhurst, who was the closest to him. Tenderly, they enwrapped one another with embraces. When he stepped back, Pastor Beveridge marveled at the quiet. Hours of waiting and worrying had drained everyone. Then people began to mill around, to express their sympathy, to try to figure out what to do next. Barbara and Don Hayhurst hung on to each other.

While this was going on inside, yet more was unfolding outside. Graef, who had arrived right behind McCarthy, was walking toward the house when Howard strode briskly down the lawn and out into the road to meet him. "John, what's going on?" Howard demanded with much frustration and more than a little anger in his voice. *"I've got to know.* Is my son dead? Are the other kids dead?" What Pastor Beveridge had just told Howard had obviously not registered.

"Howard, all the kids are dead," Graef replied.

"Thank you," Howard said. "Now I can go tell my wife."

Randy Miller, who was standing close by, marveled and thought: "There's a *strong* man." Bob put his arm over Howard's shoulder and the two men walked back up to the lawn. "I can't believe it," Howard said. McCarthy did his best to soothe Howard. After a few more minutes of aimless walking, Howard said, "I've got to go home and tell

Mary Jane. It's really going to be hard on her." Then, declining Bob's offer to take him home, Howard Borloz drove off.

Larry Carroll, Jr., was also preparing to depart—from his parents' home because his folks wanted to go to bed. After Martha went upstairs, Larry, Sr. told his son that he had not mentioned one important item to his wife because he hadn't wanted to alarm her. "I didn't tell her that Barbara had said on the phone that there were others besides Maria who had died."

When Bob McCarthy went back into the house, he learned that Walt and Connie hadn't been told about the fate of the four boys. So he went up and told them that, along with Maria, the crash had taken the lives of Tommy, Eric, Mark, and Brian. Connie screamed. She and Walt wept bitterly. ("Lord, I need your help," Bob prayed to himself.)

"Why, Bob?" Walt asked loudly. "Can you tell me *why?*"

"No, I can't" Bob said. "But I can tell you those five are in heaven. The two men in the other van are also dead. Our hearts should be going out to them. Do we know where *they* are?"

It was like a pounding surf had been stilled. Walt sat up and said, "That's right. Our five are with Jesus. The other two were also snapped up into eternity, but which way did they go?"

A few minutes later, satisfied that Walt and Connie had settled down, Bob phoned the Carrolls to inform them about their son's death. Martha, who was sitting on the edge of the bed, answered the phone. When she heard that Tommy was dead, she said, "Praise the Lord." She then asked Bob to tell Larry. Bob said: "Larry, five of our children are face to face with Jesus, and Thomas is one of them."

"Isn't God good?" Larry said. "He took my last and made him first." Neither Martha nor Larry was trying to say they were glad their son was dead. Both were merely expressing themselves in Christian terms. Martha, who had often during that night pictured her son on an operating table or maimed for life, was relieved that such worries were over. Her "Praise the Lord" comment also reflected her belief that Tommy was in heaven. Larry felt the same, and his remark that, "He took my last and made him first," alluded to the fact that Tommy, his last child, was the first of his children to die.

Mary Jane Borloz heard her husband pull into the driveway. It was not the sound she had wanted to hear. If Eric was all right, she felt

Howard would have called at once with the good news. Hearing the car instead of the phone, she reasoned, meant that he was not bringing a good report. That's why the first thing she said to Howard when she saw him was, "Eric's dead, isn't he?"

"Yes," Howard said.

"What about the others?"

"They're all gone."

"All?"

"All."

Then they embraced and wept together. Andy was in the living room with his mother when Howard told her about the accident. Although he is deaf, Andy reads lips well—and what he read on his father's lips stunned him.

"I must see Randy," Connie yelled from upstairs. *"I must see Randy."* Connie, who had been in shock since hearing of Maria's death, had been jarred back to reality when Bob had told her that the four boys had also been killed. It was as if one shock had counteracted the other. Now, for the first time, Connie "consciously knew" Maria was dead. "Was she happy tonight?" was what Connie had to find out from Randy.

"Yes, Maria was happy. She had a *really* good time." Randy knew how much his answer meant to Connie and he was glad to be able to give a reply that was both positive and honest.

Connie went to the kitchen, where she accepted Flo's offer of a cup of tea. When Connie got her tea, though, she said in her Dutch accent, "I don't take it dat vay. It's too strong." So Flo prepared her a weaker cup of tea. While Connie sipped, her son John, who had been awakened by his mother's screams, was crawling into Donna's bed with her. Soon John and Donna were asleep.

Two who were *not* asleep were Tom Cussimanio and Pierre Biscaye, who felt someone should stay the night at the house to take care of phone calls and to help in any other way possible. Pierre was responsible for a Sunday School class, so it was Tom who remained. By that hour—close to 6 A.M.—everyone else had left.

Despite the time, the Borlozes felt obliged to drive to Upper Saddle River to express their sympathy to the Van Beerses and the Hayhursts. When they arrived there, though, they saw that all the cars were gone. So Howard and Mary Jane started back home. As they neared their house, they stopped because they saw Pastor Beveridge driving toward them. The pastor, along with Reverend Wortman and Randy Miller, had stopped to have a time of prayer with the Borlozes, but had not found anyone at home. Now that they had established contact, they all went inside and poured out their hearts in prayer.

Pastor Beveridge then drove over to see the Carrolls. In front of their house, he saw Bill Carroll leaning against a telephone pole. As he said a few words to Bill, Pastor Beveridge saw tears dampening the boy's cheeks. Bill said his parents were sleeping, so Pastor Beveridge drove on.

After dropping Randy and Reverend Wortman off, Pastor Beveridge made it to his house at close to 6:45. He is, by his own admission, an emotional man. As he entered the house, he was trembling badly. With his ministerial role in the background for a short while, he no longer had to strain mightily to be Gibraltar-like. When he went into his bedroom, his wife Adele awoke and asked what had happened. While Pastor Beveridge began telling her, he took off his shoes and socks. By then, his shaking was uncontrollable. When he began crying, he crawled into bed with his clothes on. Adele put her arms around her husband, who trembled and wept and wept and wept until he went to sleep.

11

Tears and Orchids

Andy Borloz never had the privilege of hearing his brother Eric laugh. But he had *seen* him laugh. During a walk he took while Sunday's sun was chinning itself above the horizon, Andy saw Eric's laugh. Eric's face. Eric fixing Andy's car. Eric on his minibike. Memories had already begun their assault. As all the families would begin to learn that day, the mind's camera would often bring back the five youngsters with jolting effects. Andy walked on. There was, he found, no solace in any of the aspects of nature that might normally delight. A light, crisp breeze tickled the leaves and sent a few more fluttering down. Leaves. Lives.

Back at the house, Andy volunteered to assist his father with taking care of Eric's newspaper route. Howard, too, had decided this should be done. ("Occupational therapy," he thought.) As he had done hundreds of Sundays before, Howard picked up the newspapers from the distribution center and delivered them with his son. This time, though, the son at his side was Andy, not Eric.

Barbara Hayhurst had to get word to her son David, a sophomore at Rutgers. After getting the news to his roommate—Ken Knapp—via his mother, Barbara had Ken wake up David and remain at his side while she spoke with her son.

Tom Cussimanio, who had stayed at the Van Beerses, told Walt he would make all the necessary phone calls to friends and relatives to tell them about Maria. It was a task he would begin when the hour was a little more appropriate, armed with the names and numbers of those Walt had supplied. First, though, Connie made one call she felt *she* had to take care of. This was her mother's birthday and the Van Beerses had planned to drive to Long Island to celebrate the event. So Connie called her twin sister Dickie, who lived downstairs from her parents, told her about Maria, and asked to have word brought to her folks.

After having slept no more than twenty minutes, Martha and Larry Carroll got ready to go to church. As Martha left her bedroom to go downstairs, she had to walk toward Tommy's room. Instantly, she was struck by thoughts: "He is gone. I could have kept him home. I *should* have kept him home." In the breakfast room, Martha, who hadn't wept all night, broke down.

At church, Pierre Biscaye told his Sunday School class that the five youngsters had died. Then, instead of conducting his class, he and the members of that group spent all their time praying. Other changes were evident at the Pascack Bible Church that morning. The chatter among friends was replaced by brief, hushed words. Disbelief. Tears. Embraces. A solemn quiet.

David Hayhurst, who got a ride from his roommate, arrived in time to be with his parents for the church service. In the church bulletin was this item: "DON'T FORGET to hire a 'slave' from the Youth Group for your odd jobs from now to November 18th. Earnings go toward the winter retreat. For information, call Brian Hayhurst." Undoubtedly, some people must have seen that. Few, if any, probably took notice of the drawing on the front of the bulletin, a sketch that had been used for years. That drawing was by Bruce Stark, a gifted commercial artist who attends the church and who, since accepting Christ into his life, always signs his works by enlarging the "t" in his name and making it stand out like a cross. The sketch on the bulletin was of the church and some clouds. Nothing unusual. Except that above those clouds flew some birds. *Five* birds.

Throughout the day, friends, relatives and neighbors visited the four families to convey sympathy and to offer words of Christian encouragement. Connie's parents, Peter and Trudy Vander Pol, spent most of the day with the Van Beerses. Tom Cussimanio was there, too, making numerous calls, including some to each of the other three families to take care of the initial funeral arrangements. Walt and Connie expressed a desire to have Maria buried with Brian and Mark, if possible. It was possible, Tom learned, because Barbara's parents—Joseph and Edith McIlveen—had a large cemetery plot with three spaces not designated. They were agreeable to the suggestion. By the time Tom's last call was made, it was decided that Maria, Mark, and Brian would join baby Steven. A plot was located nearby for Eric and Tommy. Then, after his wife Flo had brought dinner for everyone, Tom returned home, seventeen hours after arriving at the Van Beerses' house.

The church service at seven o'clock that night consisted of a concert by Greig Beukema, his wife Sondra, and their young daughters Erika and Heidi. Beukema, who had lost his sight in 1972, had, for reasons he couldn't fathom at the time, made many changes in the songs he and his family would sing that night. It wasn't until the Beukemas drove from their home on Long Island to New Jersey that they learned of the crash. Despite not knowing beforehand, their revised program could hardly have been more appropriate, for it was accentuated by songs about how Christians can look forward to a heavenly home and about how God supplies strength in moments of need.

Among those who needed such strength that week was Pastor Beveridge. Whenever a parishioner dies, the minister has extra duties to take care of. What, then, must it be like when *five* of his flock are taken?

During the viewings on Monday and Tuesday, Pastor Beveridge shuttled between two funeral homes. There wasn't room for all five youngsters at one place, so the four boys were at the Halsey-Becker Funeral Home and Maria was a few blocks away at the Lyons Funeral Home in Westwood. The extent of the injuries sustained by the five necessitated that the viewings be closed-casket affairs. This meant that the parents and other family members were deprived of one last look at their loved ones, something that is often beneficial in establishing a sense of finality.

An article in the New York *Daily News* three days after the accident stated that a teenage girl said she had arrived at the site of the crash minutes after it had happened, that she had found Maria alive, and that she had held her in her arms while she had died. The belief that the five had died instantly had been a relief to the parents, who were thankful that their youngsters hadn't had to suffer. Thus, the article was distressing to them. The Upper Saddle River police, who had no idea this girl had been at the scene, had her come to headquarters with her parents to give a formal statement. There she admitted she had fabricated much of what she had told the press, that she had not found anyone alive.

Another of Pastor Beveridge's chores that week was "fielding the phone." Calls came from friends, concerned Christians, pastors, and reporters from coast to coast. Because of the enormity of the accident (a total of seven deaths) and a catchy human-interest twist (five youngsters had been at a Bible study), newspapers and newscasters throughout the nation carried accounts of the crash. The stickiest problem concerning the media had to do with how to handle requests from two New York City television stations wanting to cover the funeral. Pastor Beveridge's decision: The stations' mini-cam teams would be permitted only in the enclosed projection room at the back of the sanctuary and interviews could be conducted only outside the church after the service.

Out of deference to the Van Beerses, the funeral was held on Wednesday. Thursday would have been Maria's sixteenth birthday. As people entered the church for the service, which began at 1 P.M., they heard members of the youth group singing. This singing lent an ethereal touch; the youngsters, who were in a room above the sanctuary, could be heard but not seen. During the service, they sat at the front of the church, facing the audience. This day, though, there was more than the usual audience. An estimated nine hundred people—twice the normal seating capacity of the church—jammed into the pews, sat on folding chairs that had been set up, or stood in the narthex. Others spilled downstairs, where closed-circuit television had been set up.

The caskets were lined up at the front of the sanctuary—Maria's white one flanked by two bronze ones on either side. *Five* caskets. It struck people's senses. After Pastor Beveridge made a few introductory comments, Walt Van Beers stepped to the pulpit microphone and had this to say about the five:

They weren't popular in the way of the world. They turned away from alcohol. They turned away from drugs. They turned away from wild parties. They turned away from promiscuity and anything that wasn't pleasing to God. It wasn't that they didn't know these things existed. They did. But they knew they were wrong. Society will tell you that being popular, having money and power are important. God will tell you, through His son Jesus, that humility, patience, love, and concern for your brothers and sisters are far more important. So I ask you young people, in Jesus' name, that you will turn your hearts to Him and that you will seek out churches that do His name justice and deny those that don't. The denomination isn't important, but Jesus is.

We hold no bitterness in our hearts for our brothers who caused this accident and the loss of our children, and we ask you, as a body, to pray for them. And we want to say to you, Maria, to Mark, to Brian, to Eric, and to Tom that we love you, we're glad you're with the Lord, and we praise Him for that.

Randy Miller began by quoting John 3:16 and, because he had spent much of Saturday evening with the youngsters, was able to add some touching insights:

> "For God so loved the world, that he gave his only begotten Son, that whosoever believeth in him should not perish, but have everlasting life." God *is real.* The lives of these kids proved this to me. . . . I can't help but think of the changed lives that have occurred, and will continue to occur, through the witness of these kids. Their attitude can best be epitomized by a song we sang at least twice that night with enthusiasm and conviction and joy and praise to our God. . . . Listen to the words:

> Yes my God is real
> I can feel Him deep in my soul
> Every day, He says to me,
> "Child, don't worry. *I* have control."
> He took the victory from the grave
> He's the only one that saves you. Yeah.
> Yes, my God, He knows
> Just how much we all can bear
> And when our burdens get too heavy
> Oh, the Lord will be right there
> He'll make all right
> All your toil and your strife and your worry.
> Yes my God is real
> I can feel Him deep in my soul
> Every day, He says to me,
> "Child, don't worry. *I* have control."

Bonnie Furman, one of the hardest-working members of the youth group, was the next to speak. What Bonnie did was introduce a song that the young people were about to sing—"For Those Tears I Died"—Maria's favorite.

As he approached the microphone to read his *Meditations of A Father,* Don Hayhurst sighed and uttered this brief, soft prayer: "Lord, help me to get through this." The Lord got him through it. Understandably, Walt Van Beers had labored when he had spoken and Don did, too, his own words arousing his emotions. Here are his *Meditations:*

> In my home lived two angels. No, they couldn't have been because they were flesh of my flesh. They were saints. How, Lord, can a saint be a

loud noise covered with grease and dirt? But then, you look on the inside, don't you? . . .

Now I understand, Lord. I understand a lot of things. I understand the spirit that burned in those boys. Oh, it wasn't that I didn't appreciate them in their natural ways, for I had come to truly savor their presence in my home as they filled it with their fun and jokes, with their love of life and living, with their house-shaking frolicking as they tested and then enjoyed just being alive.

But I now understand that which burned from out of their spirits—spirits that had been reborn by your touch, Lord Jesus, when they came to put their trust in you. Oh—I could see some years ago that their spirits had been born anew—but there was that certain driving fire that kept showing itself from time to time until it became apparent more recently that it was becoming a roaring fire, thus becoming the controlling force in their lives. Why, it's You, Lord. I recognize You there. It was Your presence that entered in as a flicker that day that their spirits were reborn.

And now I see You putting it all together for me to understand. Now I understand why their fighting and arguing with each other seemed to fade away—in Brian as he got caught up in living for others and in Mark as he suddenly grew older as he faced You and Your priorities in Latin America this summer. I realize now how much You even used that lime explosion in Honduras that sprayed Mark's body and eyes. How his words burn in my heart as I remember him saying that as he returned from the river where he attempted to wash the lime away that the continuing of the burning in his eyes caused him to think—to face something about himself. And that was that he didn't really have to worry, even if he was going to have to lose his sight, because he belonged to You, Lord, and that You could be trusted to look out for his life and that nothing else really mattered anyway. . . .

Brian was a new member in choir and we noted through the week that he couldn't get Sunday's anthem out of his mind: "How Lovely is Thy Dwelling Place." When the boys left for their meeting, I discovered that each of them had left their sneakers lined up in their rooms, with the laces neatly tied. Did the Lord help the boys get their houses put in order? I feel that He did.

I'll just say this about those kids, as it is said in Proverbs: "A man is known by his actions." Their lives were examples of the love of Jesus in action. Oscar Hammerstein wrote:

A bell is no bell till you ring it.
A song is no song till you sing it.
And love in your heart wasn't put there to stay.
Love isn't love till you give it away.

And those kids were giving it away, and now they are with the Father and Jesus.

The apostle Paul said, "I want you to realize that God has been made rich because we who are Christ's have been given to Him." Does God actually have a need? Certainly He does. His need was that man would share His life. And God loved us so much that He gave His son Jesus to die so that we (whoever would be willing) would share His life. That happens when we put our trust in Jesus—as the kids did—and He then touches our spirit (the real me, down deep inside) and our spirit is reborn (born again).

Pastor Beveridge then said a few words about each of the five youngsters, after which he added some personal reflections about the accident, and his beliefs about death and God's promises:

When I first met Maria three years ago, she was probing and making new discoveries. About the most significant discovery she made was to see the faith of her mother and father turn to Jesus Christ. Walt and Connie, you have committed to her the most important thing that could be committed to any of our children—a commendable faith. . . . Eric, a silent member sometimes . . . . There was always lurking behind that quiet facade a great deal of life and we learned to appreciate him as he thrust his shoulder to the work of our young people. Tommy was a child saint. He ministered with the strength of someone who had known the Lord for years and years. . . . Mark used to needle me incessantly. . . . I marveled at what the Lord did in his life in a very short period. Mark grew like wildfire in the last few months. Brian was kind of quiet, except when he was throwing a Frisbee around the parking lot or yelling and screaming with the rest of the kids and enjoying life. I'll always remember how he always needed the key to the church for something or other. He was always looking for *my* sponges to use on the days of car washes. . . . But the most important thing was that they loved Jesus. Last Saturday night they began their lives in heaven with that Jesus. . . . We have no doubt where they are. We have *no* doubt. . . .

When Jesus went to Lazarus' grave and met Mary and Martha. . . . He was touched by the human condition. The Scriptures tell us He wept. He *knows* the pain you are going through, *all* of you. He has been there, He has observed grief, and His heart has melted with grief.

Humanly speaking, on the cross He said, "My God, my God, why hast thou forsaken me?" He could have, as the Scripture tells us, called forth a legion of angels to deliver Him from that circumstance, but He limited Himself to the human experience so that He would *know* what you're going through. You have a Jesus who understands. He didn't take those kids lightly. Their homegoing was not just a flippant response of some vindictive God who snatches away to make us cry. But, at the same time that He was joyful about their homecoming, He was grieving with you and He said, "Don't worry, I'll comfort you. Let not your heart be troubled. You who believe in God, believe also in me. Dry your tears. I am with you."

Saturday night, as Pierre Biscaye and I returned from the scene of the accident . . . and had to go back and say, "None of them lived," I was in such a conflict of emotions going back in that car that I welled up with sorrow and sometimes bitterness and sometimes anguish. I felt somehow overwhelmed at that moment and I remember, as clearly as I've remembered anything in my life, *"If Jesus isn't, then life is not worth living one more minute. . . ."* If there is no sense to Jesus, there's no sense to life. I would not want to live one day longer with the pain that this life can throw on us if it were not for the fact that Jesus Christ has won every battle and He says, "Hold tight. I'm still behind everything, in control of everything, and I care for you. . . ."

Everybody then sang "What a Friend We Have In Jesus." When it was time for the last stanza, there was a sudden silence—a hush. *Everyone* stopped singing. Disbelief had stilled the throng. Standing behind the microphone was Barbara Hayhurst. She had sung many a soprano solo, but it was almost impossible to believe that this woman, who had just lost her two youngest sons, intended to sing *now*. Pastor Beveridge was surprised when he saw her leave her pew and walk up next to him. When Barbara told him she wanted to sing, he asked, "Alone?" She replied, "Yes." Sing she did, with a remarkably controlled voice.

In his closing remarks, Pastor Beveridge addressed himself "as pastor and minister and friend" to the eight parents. "Listen to this as if Jesus were right here speaking to you," he told them. "He says, 'I am the resurrection and the life'; Connie and Walt, Don and Barbara, Howard and Mary Jane, Martha and Larry. 'He that believeth in me, though he were dead, yet shall he live. Don't be troubled. You believe in God, believe also in me. In my Father's house are many mansions; if it were not so, I would have told you. I go to prepare a place for you. And if I go . . . I will come again, and receive you unto myself, that where I am, there you may be also.' And He says to you Walt and Connie, Don and Barbara, Howard and Mary Jane, Larry and Martha, to all of you who grieve, 'Peace I leave with you, my peace I give unto you; not as the world giveth, give I unto you. Let not your heart be troubled, neither let it be afraid.' Lord bless you."

Then the five caskets were wheeled up the aisle and out of the sanctuary. Many people who had held together emotionally until then found that this sight prompted tears over which they had no control. Larry Carroll, Jr., who was standing a few feet from Pastor Beveridge, suggested that a song be sung to "get our eyes back on Jesus." Pastor chose not a song but a chorus familiar to those in his congregation and the people joined with him in singing with tenderness, "He is Lord. He is Lord. He is risen from the dead and He is Lord. Every knee shall bow, every tongue confess that Jesus Christ is Lord."

It was a gray, dank day, the kind that added its own heaviness to the service held that afternoon at George Washington Memorial Park in Paramus. The service was brief. What more could be said?

Reverend Wortman had given a copy of the following letter to the parents earlier in the week:

> I just want to write this note to say that I talked with Mrs. Harlan Stricklett today (mother of Roger and Stuart). She was wanting to get in touch with someone at Pascack Bible Church to express their sympathy. . . . She told me several times, "Tell the parents we are praying for them." They have attended Archer United Methodist Church in Allendale for fourteen years. Their two sons and daughter were active in the Youth Fellowship of that church. . . . Let us ask the Lord what expression of love He would have us take toward this family.

At eight o'clock that Wednesday, there was a memorial service for Roger and Stuart in their church. (The bodies of the two men had already been cremated.) More than two hundred fifty people were at the service that evening, among them, the parents of the other five youngsters. Don Hayhurst, impressed by Reverend Wortman's letter, had suggested that they attend as a group. Don spoke briefly with Harlan Stricklett and said a few words of prayer before he and the other parents left.

Going to that service was not easy for the parents, who were already emotionally wrung out. Such acts, though, were uncommonly common that week. Another instance of this sort involved Rob Grieve and Bonnie Furman. Rob, remembering that Brian had all the financial records for the youth group with him on Saturday night and knowing how vital they were, felt he had an obligation to fulfill: He had to retrieve those ledgers from the remains of the Hayhurst van. Rob, who wasn't old enough to drive, needed a ride to the salvage yard where the van had been taken. It was Bonnie who drove him there a few days after the accident. One look at that vehicle was enough to give them the jitters, but Rob poked around among the wreckage and found some of Maria's jewelry, an assortment of books—and the financial records.

No less easy in its own way was the baptismal service eight days after the crash. Maria, Brian, and Tommy were to have been baptized that day. Greg Bunce, a member of the youth group, wrote a song in memory of the five and he sang it at that service for the young people. Part of that song included these three lines: "Though they may not be at our side/They'll be with us in memory/Even when our tears have dried."

When it came time to handle the insurance claims for the accident, the eight parents went to Dick Heck, a member of their church. Heck, a realtor who had been out of the insurance business for several years, consented to help. "The only thing they asked for was coverage of out-of-pocket expenses," Heck recalls. "There was no concern about any payment for the loss of the children or for the pain and suffering the families had gone through. That's where the *big* money would have been, but they decided it would be a part of their united testimony not to hold any animosity or to make any effort to grab the opportunity to make a lot of money off the situation. The insurance investigators who handled the case were flabbergasted by this Christian attitude."

There was no doubt the four families could have pocketed bundles of money from the company that insured the other van in the accident. In addition to evidence that had been obtained earlier, there was a report on the alcohol tests that had been run on all seven people in the crash. Absolutely no trace of alcohol was found in the five teenagers. To begin to grasp the meaning of the reports on the men in the other van, one must first know that, according to New Jersey law, anyone with an alcohol level of 0.1 or higher is considered to be intoxicated. Tests showed that Stuart Stricklett, the passenger in the other vehicle, had an alcohol level of 0.236. For Roger Stricklett, who was driving, the reading was 0.216.

And then there were the orchids. Clifford Mohwinkel and his wife Anita have for years had a small greenhouse on their property in Westwood. The flowers they grew were lovely, but nothing out of the ordinary—until a few days after the accident. That's when the Mohwinkels counted an unusual number of orchids that had blossomed simultaneously: One, two, three, four, five.

"It was an absolute miracle that five blooms opened at the same time," Clifford says. "We have never before had that many at once and we have never had that many at one time since," Anita adds. "It was a phenomenon. There were three white orchids and two purples."

At first, the Mohwinkels were delighted by this rarity. This feeling was quickly transcended by a feeling of wonder when they realized how significant the number five was at that particular time. Thus, Clifford and Anita, members of the Pascack Bible Church, saw to it that, along with Thanksgiving baskets that were being given to the four families, went the five orchids—one each to the Van Beerses, Borlozes, and Carrolls, and two to the Hayhursts.

12

Oaks of Righteousness

"If this book is going to have a ministry, it will have to show us as we were, as we are now and the different routes we've taken during this healing process. It's also going to have to show our humanness."—Walt Van Beers

"I don't feel we would be honest if we hid our struggles and just pointed out the high points all of us have had in our battles with our emotions. It's important for us to share what we were like at our worst, because this has been part of it all. Other people have to be able to see that."—David Hayhurst

"The thing is, some of us may not yet be willing to share those 'down' times."—Howard Borloz

"All of us [the eight parents] met and talked about these things and about whether or not it was the Lord's will to do this book. We realized it would be painful to recall many of these things. There were many questions we had to ask ourselves and which we had to pray about. Did we want to go through bringing back painful memories? Did we want to expose ourselves and those we are so close to? Would all of this be of real help to others?"—Walt Van Beers

"I don't know if I'll ever be able to talk about some things."—Martha Carroll

"An honest portrayal of me cannot be all that sweet."—Mary Jane Borloz

"The idea is to convey help to others. To do that, people will have to be able to relate to us."—Howard Borloz

"We're going to have to ask the Lord for His guidance through all of this."—Don Hayhurst

Those comments were among many in June of 1979 at the first meeting with the four families to discuss the advisability of doing this book. Seven of the eight parents and David Hayhurst were gathered that evening in the Hayhurst home. Larry Carroll, who was recuperating from extensive surgery, was the only parent unable to attend. It was explained that the book would not be done unless *all eight* shared the certainty that it was the Lord's will to do so. An informal survey of opinions that night indicated that no more than three parents felt led to proceed with such a book. That seemed to be the end of that. No attempt was made to stay in contact with the families. Only one link existed between all the parties concerned: prayer. Several weeks later, Don Hayhurst phoned to say, "We've all prayed about the matter and it's been explained to Larry Carroll. All eight of us now feel the Lord is directing us toward proceeding with the book."

Thus, the work proceeded. Some delays were unavoidable, but others were part of an attempt to provide a rather long-range view of the grieving process over three and a half years.

From the outset, it was felt that a major strength of this book would be that it would draw upon the views of eight parents, not merely one, as do most such books. This increases the chance for strong reader identification, that link that should help draw you close to one or more of the eight because of a sense of identity or kinship you will feel.

If you expect to read about eight people who coped with grief in majestic and all-victorious ways, you are in for a letdown. You won't be disappointed, though, if you are longing to read about men and women who are sincere and honest enough to admit that they have walked down long paths, *very* long paths. All eight proved themselves to be, as Isaiah 61:3 says of those who mourn, "oaks of righteousness."

Barbara and Donald Hayhurst

Back in 1682, the first Hayhurst, a Quaker minister, came to America. Later generations eventually moved to the Midwest. There, in Kankakee, Illinois, Donald Hayhurst was born in 1929. His growing-up years were spent in Momence, a town of some three thousand inhabitants located fifty miles south of Chicago.

"I attended a church that taught salvation, but I never made a commitment to the Lord until I was a senior in high school," Don Hayhurst points out. "It was my grandmother—my mom's mother—who led me to the Lord. She had a *loving* relationship with the Lord." Don is a calm, easy-going man who uses low-key words and who almost never gives extra emphasis to any of them, but *"loving"* was a word he stressed. Don went on with his recollections: "After I'd come to the Lord, I'd go to her house and she would eagerly say to me, 'Let's gossip about Jesus.' "

Barbara was born and reared in Bergen County, New Jersey. She and Don met while both were attending Moody Bible Institute in Chicago in 1953. It seemed highly improbable they would ever marry, for Barbara had a steady boyfriend back home and Don was engaged to a girl he had met while stationed at Fort Eustis, Virginia during his two-year hitch in the army.

But strange twists do many tales take. Twist No. 1: Don's engagement was severed. Twist No. 2: Barbara and her boyfriend stopped dating each other. Twist No. 3: While visiting an aunt and uncle in Norfolk, Virginia, after graduating from Moody, Don wrote to Barbara. "She had told me that if I was ever in her area I should stop in for a visit," Don explains. Virginia is not exactly around the corner from northeastern New Jersey, but when you're young and an idea gets lodged in your mind, you don't allow geography to be a drag. Besides, if twists of fate don't come your way, it is often possible to do some twisting of your own if there is sufficient motivation. No sooner did Barbara's return letter (complete with an invitation) arrive than Don felt motivated to zip off to New Jersey. Twist No. 4: During Don's weeklong visit with Barbara and her parents, Barbara just happened to be home, thanks to a back injury that had kept her out of work all summer.

Then some of that fate-twisting help was given during the next few months. Barbara became a stewardess with Capitol Airlines. What good did it do to be a stewardess? Well, Barbara put in an application to be assigned to Capitol's staff in Chicago; if it was approved she wouldn't be too far from Don. It was almost Christmas when Don received a call from Barbara about the verdict on where she would be stationed. "As soon as she said it was Chicago, I knew that was *it*," Don says.

The twists that led to bringing Don and Barbara together were replaced, so to speak, by straight roads that led right to the altar in June of 1957. Despite having sent out applications to numerous churches for a job as director of Christian education, Don had been unable to secure such a position. As a result, Barbara and Don moved to New Jersey two years after becoming Mr. and Mrs. There Don got a job as a carpenter and in June of '59 began working for Art Wire/Doduco, where he is now the manager of purchasing.

Their first child, Corinne (pronounced Kuh-RINN), was born in Illinois in May 1958. During their first five years in New Jersey, the Hayhursts had four more children: David (August 1959), twins Brian and Steven (September 1961), and Mark (February 1963). Don and Barbara can now chuckle about the rough and tumble shenanigans of their children and about the Avon saleslady who, Barbara says, "loved to come to our house because there was always something going on that she could tell her family about at the dinner table." What may well have been that woman's favorite firsthand Hayhurst story had to do with the time that Mark, then four years old, marched past her without so much as a thread of clothes on. Mark was carrying his soaking-wet clothing and was on his way to find a bathing suit, the better to plunge back into the chilly little backyard goldfish pond where he and several other children were trying to catch the one finny resident thereof.

Time. It has a way of softening many of yesterday's hurts. Some pains, though, are too intense. They scar the memory just as surely as a deep cut does the flesh. It was not merely the domino-like way that illness struck the Hayhurst house as it does in any large family. No, it went far beyond that. Beyond the nine months of illness that Barbara suffered through with each of her four pregnancies. Beyond the eye troubles that began for Barbara when she was about fifteen years old. There were other tribulations. "When Corinne was five months old, she had asthmatoid bronchitis with pneumonia and was in an oxygen tent," Barbara says. After a sigh, she continues: "Corinne spent her whole first winter on antibiotics, finally getting hives after each dosage. We had this terrifying feeling that we were going to lose her."

Then there was the radiator. It was disconnected and stood near the back door, outside of the Hayhursts' house in Westwood. Obviously, that was a dangerous place for a radiator. So, to make certain it wouldn't fall on someone, Don lugged it away from there. He was not able, however, to lift the heavy radiator into the car trunk so it could be hauled away. Thus, the radiator was placed along the driveway until someone could give Don a hand with getting rid of it. The radiator wasn't there long before five-year-old Corinne monkeyed with it and had it fall on her left foot. Corinne's screams brought Barbara, who took one look at her daughter's trapped foot and knew what she *had* to do. With one mighty heave, Barbara lifted the radiator. Corinne had a crushed instep and two broken toes. As for Barbara, she hurt her shoulder and back lifting that radiator and to this day is still treated for the damage that was done.

There was still more. Brian, who was three months old, came down with a cold. While putting Steven, the other twin, to bed on the night of December 27, 1961, Barbara heard him "breathing funny" and thought to herself, "Oh, don't tell me you're coming down with a cold, too." When Don and Barbara got up the next morning, they checked on the twins. Brian was fine. Steven had stopped breathing but was still warm.

"The doctor told us there was nothing we could have done," Barbara says. "Don tried mouth-to-mouth resuscitation for a long time. When the ambulance got there, the attendants saw he was doing it right, so they told him to keep trying. But when the doctor arrived he told Don it was no use. The doctor explained that even if we had been next to Steven all night long it would have been hard to have saved him because they found he had a kind of pneumonia that hits the lungs in such a way that they fill with liquid in minutes and causes the person to quickly choke to death. After we knew Steven was dead, I sat and held him in my arms for the last time.

"Because of premenstrual tension and everything else, I never came off the wall," Barbara adds with a shake of her head. *"Never.* I was going into depression. We were screaming at each other *all the time.* Finally, my doctor performed a hysterectomy to get me off the wall. Troubles kept piling up and Don and I kept screaming at each other. I was cracking up. How can you tell people, especially ones you've gone to church with all your life, that your marriage is falling apart?"

"People at church showed love," Don says. "They'd inquire about how we were. After a few weeks, you feel guilty telling people you're still hurting. So you say, 'Oh, we're fine, thanks.' There were pressures at work. There were problems with handling the kids, problems with the marriage, physical problems, money problems. All those things left me feeling like I was trapped in a box from which I couldn't escape. Then Barbara and I had the biggest blowout we ever had. When things quieted down that night, we came to an agreement that we had to do *something."*

Lest one think that the Hayhurst spats were minor tiffs, Barbara contributes the following: "We had some *real goodies.* We shouted and screamed so loud that I wouldn't have been surprised if everyone in the neighborhood heard every word. Larry and Martha Carroll live right next door to us and I can only imagine what they must have thought," Barbara says as she scrunches up her shoulders and shudders.

The Carrolls heard enough to prompt them to pray extra hard for the Hayhursts. They also got them to attend Bible studies on Monday nights at their house. Not long after that, the Hayhursts were "baptized in the Holy Spirit."

Don says of this experience: "When we left the Carrolls' house that night, we both felt a peace and we could tell that a tremendous cleansing was taking place. So much of our spiritual life had become mechanical and dry, but from that night on we had an insatiable hunger for God's Word, for prayer, and for quiet meditation."

For a number of years, the Hayhursts were busily engaged in an extensive ministry that included the taping of various meetings and speakers, editing tapes for use on radio programs, plus duplicating and distributing tapes, often in large quantities. It was a workload that turned out to be too much for Don, whose health suffered. Reluctantly, the Hayhursts dropped their taping ministry.

Because of the lateness of the accident on Saturday night, it was not until Monday that *The Record* carried stories about it. One of that day's two front-page stories about the crash was headlined:

Father:
'They're
with
Jesus'

Those words were excerpted from what Don had said to a reporter about the fate of the five youngsters who had been in the Hayhurst van: "We're confident and pleased to know where they are. They're with Jesus." At the time of the accident, Don was forty-nine years old, Barbara forty-three.

Who—Christian or not—could have read Don's words in *The Record* and not have been impressed by the firmness of his belief? Those who heard Barbara sing at the funeral service—her voice steady, clear, unchoked—were also uplifted.

Despite a sleepless night, on the morning after the accident, Barbara was able to think clearly enough to display her concern about how to break the news of the death of Mark and Brian to those who had to be told. She arranged to have David's roommate at his side when she phoned him. She also figured out a way to enlist the aid of another couple to be with her parents when she called them on Sunday morning.

Eight months after the accident, Don Hayhurst said, "For years I'd leaned on Romans 8:28 and had often quoted it to others about how 'we know that all things work together for good to them that love God.' It was a verse I used to say to people who had troubles. My general attitude was, 'Cheer up, brother, all things are great.' But now when I thought about Romans 8:28 or heard someone else use it, I had to say, 'Hey, wait a minute. Last November eleventh wasn't great for our family or for the other three families.' I was saying to myself, *Are things really working together for my good, for our good? Are they?* A couple days ago, I was looking at pictures of Brian and Mark. I had just come into the house and when I saw their pictures I said, 'You really *aren't* coming back, are you?' That was the first time I truly realized they were gone. Recovering from the loss of the boys is more than forcing yourself to say, 'Life must go on.' We had to reach the point where we could fully believe the Father would put our new lives together and that we could trust Him to do so."

Judging from what Don had to say, he'd struggled with his grief but now had it well in hand. Why shouldn't he have it under control? After all, he was a man who had been walking close to the Lord for years and he was one of the most respected laymen in the church. Besides, he'd had *eight full months* in which to take care of his sorrowing. It sounds rather simple when reduced to those terms. *Was* it that simple? Barbara Hayhurst knew it wasn't. This was obvious when she pointed out that, "I'd wake up and hear my husband sobbing in his sleep or in Mark's old room sobbing for answers while on his knees."

A year and a half after the loss of his two sons, Don was in a reflective mood and spoke about how, for a long time, it was sounds that brought flashbacks of Mark and Brian. While at work, Don frequently heard a nearby train. "Whenever I would hear that train and its whistle, I would always think of Mark because he used to like trains so much," Don said almost solemnly. "Most of all, though, it was music that would stir up memories. Nothing seemed to be important to me after the accident and the memories that came weren't always pleasant. A year after the accident, there was a memorial service at the church. When I got home that night, I looked at the pictures of Brian and Mark in my den, which used to be Mark's room. While I looked at those pictures, I realized that the 'caring' hurt was still there and that I certainly missed the boys. But I also realized that the 'tearing' hurt was gone.

"My faith in the Lord is as strong as ever and there's a quality of determination that goes with it now. This is a determination that comes from a belief that God will not let Satan win in this matter of grieving.

I would like to think that the devil is looking at four families from our church who lost youngsters in the accident and that he's finding out that they are stubborn people—stubbornly determined in their faith because they have invested in it and they are not going to back away from it. I think if this is saying anything it is not that we are super-spiritual people, but that we have been upheld by the body of Christ as it has ministered to us. The prayers and support of the body have brought all of us through."

Slightly more than three years after the crash, he again assessed his situation. "After the accident, my first reaction was that I felt I'd been kicked in the stomach," he began. "I didn't understand the tragedy, but I felt I had to be God's man. I threw myself into my work and got overly involved in church duties by being both an undershepherd and a youth elder. The second year, I felt upset because I didn't get the input I expected from the Lord. It was just that I was trying to do too much. It held back my recovery. Increased demands at work and church left me almost like a vegetable. My spiritual antennae weren't up and I wasn't sensitive to the Lord. I didn't give Him a chance to be a healer.

"Just a little while before the accident, I was with the group of undershepherds and my heart was crying out to walk more closely with Him and to know Him better. I cried out so that the whole Fellowship Hall was filled with my voice, 'Let it be, Lord. I want to walk with you.' It's taken three years for me to recover enough so that I've almost made it back to the place where I was then. There hasn't been any growth, just a getting back. I felt that something inside me had died, but now I'm content to leave it all to the Lord so that He can handle things. What you don't realize when you're going through something like this is that you get in your own way. After I dropped a lot of my duties at church, that made '81 like a year of rejuvenation in which I felt a new closeness with the Lord. At the end of almost three years, you wonder how many times the memories of the accident can come up and *still* be so excruciating. Now they are more like fond memories about the boys. Some day I will be the Lord's man again in whatever way He wants to use me."

Barbara Hayhurst is no mere five-footer; she is five feet one-half inch tall, and mighty proud of that half inch. The cream that tops off her perky personality is the animation she adds to her conversation— hands poking and stroking the air, voice rising and falling in keeping with her moods, head bobbing, fingers dancing or wiggling. These and other gestures are her way of giving her listeners a chance to use their eyes as well as their ears.

"It hurt me after the funeral service when people would come up to me days and weeks later and say, 'You were *so strong* to be able to sing that way,'" Barbara said eight months later. "*I* wasn't strong. It was God who gave me some of *His* strength. I wasn't upset with the people who thought it was me. I was upset because God wasn't being given the credit. To get up and sing the way I did seemed like a dumb thing to do, a showy thing. I've always had a hangup about things like that. All I know is that I had this feeling that I *had* to do it. I didn't understand why until after the service. That's when Howard Borloz told me that he had wanted to ask me to sing but that he couldn't bring himself to do it at that time. Apparently, his desire was so strong that the Lord answered it and gave me the strength I needed at that moment."

Barbara was not fully swept up in the grieving process for at least eight months, mostly because she had been so involved in preparing for her daughter's wedding, which took place seven months after the crash. "The wedding was in June," Barbara said a year after that event. "In September, David went back to college. All of a sudden, I was alone. There had been so much to do to get ready for the wedding that it postponed normal mourning for me. When everyone was gone and things settled down, *then* I discovered how *drastically* my life had been changed. There was an aimlessness to my life. I was not sure where I fit in, what I should do. The second year has been harder than the first. I look around and say, 'Where do I go from here, God?'

"There are times when you think you're doing fine and then all of a sudden [her right hand swishes in front of her face] you get knocked down, and you're not even sure of what happened to you or what caused it. I believe that you must ask every day for the Lord to fill you *that* day, to show you where you are supposed to be so He can lead you. If you don't do that, you are going to grow spiritually cold. The mother part of me wants Brian and Mark back, but another part of me *knows* that they are with their Lord and that in His presence they are more content than if they were here. That does not change the fact that I still hurt, though. If I didn't know my children were with the Lord, I don't think I could handle *that.*"

September 29, 1980 was a special day for the Hayhursts; on that day they became grandparents for the first time. Little Christopher was born to Corinne and Ben Nelson. Thus, September 29th would always carry a double significance for Barbara and Don, for it had been exactly nineteen years earlier that Brian and Steven had been born.

By the time a little more than three years had elapsed since the crash, Barbara's battle with grief seemed to have worn her down considerably. Her bounciness was less evident and her smiles, when they did arrive, did not stick around as long as they once did. It was at this juncture that she said: "It seems that other people feel, 'It's been a year or two since the accident. I'm *sure* they're doing fine by *now*.' Well, I'm not fine even now. About all I can say is, 'What am I here for? What's the purpose of my living?' There are times when I'm *completely* overcome by my emotions even without a memory coming to mind. I had Steven only three months and it took me five years to get over his loss. I had Brian seventeen years and Mark fifteen. What do I expect?"

13

Mary Jane and Howard Borloz

"It's not that you haven't faced reality, but it takes time before the day comes when it finally sinks in that your child is *never ever* going to walk through the front door of your house again," Mary Jane Borloz said in June of 1979. "We have a friend who lost a child a few years before Eric died. She did very well, but it just seemed she hung on to her grief longer than I thought she should have. Never having lost a child of my own at that time, I was judging her. Then Eric died. Until you go through it yourself, you can't *really* know what it's like. I called up that other mother then and told her, '*Now* I understand.' "

That was the same evening that Howard Borloz said, "I defy anyone to say how long it takes to get over an emotional situation like this. Some things are hard to explain. Like my attitude about pizza. Eric used to order pizza so often. I haven't had a piece since the accident and I don't think I ever will. I'm sure there are some people who can't figure out what all of us [the eight parents] are going through, who can't understand the situation at all. Through it all, one verse has helped me more than any other: 'Lean not unto thine own understanding' [Proverbs 3:5]. There's more in that chapter that means a lot to me. And I've also been helped by the verses that say, 'Be anxious for nothing, but in everything, by prayer and supplication with thanksgiving, let your requests be made known unto God. And the peace of God, which passeth all understanding, shall keep your hearts and minds through Christ Jesus' [Philippians 4:6,7, New Scofield Reference Bible]." One footnote: Less than two months earlier, Howard had undergone surgery for chest cancer. He did not say a word about it that night. It was not until two-and-a-half years later that Howard mentioned his operation, and then it was only in reply to direct questions about it.

"Yes. Yes. There was surgery." Judging from the dispassionate tone

127

with which he spoke, one might have thought he was talking about having an operation for the removal of an eyelash. "It was in early May 1979. Nothing unusual about it at all," he went on, adding nothing more than a half-shrug and a slight raising of his eyebrows. That's his way of saying, "No big deal." Howard concluded his abbreviated explanation of his surgery by saying, "No follow-up therapy. No chemotherapy. No adverse effects except when the weather changes."

When talking about the Borlozes, a few people used the term "stoic," particularly in reference to Howard. The Borlozes are, in reality, far from stoical. To spend any time with Howard and Mary Jane, and to listen to them talk about Eric is to begin to appreciate that they have hurt as much as anyone else. Then why do some people consider them to be stoics? Probably because few people have spent much time trying to help the Borlozes with their anguish. And because almost all of the grieving done by Mary Jane and Howard has been done privately. Added to that is the fact that the Borlozes are not as much in the mainstream of the church as are the other three couples. A fourth reason they are regarded by some people as being stoical is that the Borlozes don't *appear* to be suffering. The strength they display in public is very real; it can also be very misunderstood.

It seems aptly symbolic that Howard Borloz, so much of whom lies beneath the surface, is a former submariner. One will not find much of Howard by skimming through shallow water with the periscope up, for he keeps much of himself many fathoms down. His conversations border on being elegant and eloquent. When Howard gets into one of those E and E grooves, his ever-so-precise pronunciation becomes even more apparent because he seems to bite off each syllable of each word. This distinctive aspect of his slightly-slower-than-average speech makes it almost seem that every syllable arrives at the listener's ear via special delivery. Furthermore, Howard's sentences are often deftly constructed, so much so that one can almost see the punctuation marks spilling forth from his lips. Added to all of that is his choice of words, a selection that at times is refreshingly out of the ordinary. In short, it is a delight to listen to Howard Borloz talk.

Even though sons Steven and Eric used to kid their father about his speech mannerisms, Howard remained undaunted and unchanged. What is important to grasp here is that those are characteristics of much of his life, not merely his way of defending the way he talks. Another thing about Howard that has remained unchanged is his crewcut hair, which he maintains he has "always" had. Even he, however, would admit to one change: Among the headful of upright strands there is now more salt than pepper.

Two days after the accident, Howard said this about Eric to a reporter from *The Record:* "He was just an average boy. He was not outstanding in anything, but had many varied interests. We are all of the belief that he's gone on to something better than this." Howard has an aversion to boasting. Deep within him, however, there may well be deserved feelings that Eric was more than "just an average boy." One of Howard's favorite stories about Eric concerns the day his son and a young friend joined Howard aboard the *U.S.S. Ling,* a submarine that had been brought to the Hackensack River in nearby Hackensack as a tourist attraction. Howard was for a time a volunteer guide on the *Ling.*

"While I went about serving as a guide, Eric and his friend roamed around the *Ling* on their own," Howard begins. "One of the other men assumed the boys were potential souvenir hunters, so he told them they would have to leave. Eric later told me that he said to the man, 'In that case, you'll have to put my father off, too.' He was delighted to be able to say that and when he told me about the incident Eric said it was a 'neat' feeling to be able to say that, to be able to make his point without being smart-alecky about it."

A small incident, to be sure. But Howard Borloz delights in small treasures. As he recounted this tale a trace of a smile appeared on his face. It was as if Howard would like to have turned on a broad grin but was suppressing the urge because a full-blown smile might have indicated that he was overly proud of Eric. Pride, like boastfulness, is to be consigned to Davey Jones' locker, Howard believes. What would he have boasted about if he had permitted himself such a luxury? Well, he could have boasted about his relationship with Eric, which was warm and tender and filled with mutual respect. Howard could also have bragged about how well disciplined his son was, about how polite he was, about how handsome he was. Or Howard might have mentioned how good it made him feel to know that his son was proud of the fact that his dad had been aboard submarines during World War II.

The war. This is Howard's staccato-type summation of his career as a submariner: "I was stationed in the Asiatic-Pacific theater of war. Yes, I was involved in combat. I was part of the original crew of the

U.S.S. Shark II in New London, Connecticut. We took her out on a shakedown cruise through the Panama Canal and to the Pacific. We made two successful patrol runs, sinking Japanese tonnage. In crew rotation, I was taken off the *Shark* along with eleven others at Pearl Harbor. I was bitterly disappointed about that. The *Shark* went out again and was lost. It was never heard from again. I was put aboard the *Dragonet* and made two more successful patrols. I was a gunner's mate. It's all team effort. As for me being personally responsible for the demise of any of the enemy. . . ," Howard trailed off with a half-closing of his eyes and a half-shrug.

Howard then added this afterthought: "Ironically, I'm now working with Japanese and I've gone to school for four semesters while struggling to learn their language." Howard helps run the huge printing presses at *The Record,* has been to Japan to learn about the processes there, and has shared his knowledge with those Japanese who have come to the U.S. to further *their* expertise.

"We met during the war," says Mary Jane, whose maiden name was Blundell. "I was going out with a friend of his who was on the same sub. After Howard and I started dating, his sub was gone for a year and a half. Two years after Howard returned we became engaged. We were married in 1948. Both of us grew up in this part of Jersey. I was born in Chicago but was raised in Hackensack. Howard is from Teaneck. When we were first married, we used to go to my sister's place to watch television because we didn't have a set of our own. Then we bought *our own* little TV. Our first house was in Hackensack and cost us $4,800. Howard said he wanted to build his own house. I didn't want him to do it because he was putting in so many hours at work. But I told him, 'If you build it, I'll live in it.' He built it in six months and we've lived here since 1954."

The Borlozes had three sons. Steven is five years older than Andy. Eric was the "caboose papoose" who came along eight years after Andy.

"When Andy was six months old, I *knew* he was deaf," Mary Jane says.

"We took him to New York to a Dr. Fowler, who was the best in his field on the east coast," Howard adds. "While we sat in his office, Dr. Fowler told us, 'The problem is not that Andy is deaf. There's nothing you can do about *that.* The problem is that you, as the parents, have to learn to accept the fact that Andy is deaf. If you can't accept that, then you'll have to do something about it if you want to be of help to him.' What Dr. Fowler was telling us was that many parents who have handicapped children suffer from a trauma that is so great that they can't handle it and can't be of help to the children. You can *not* possibly explain what this experience is like. You have to live through it to understand it. Andy made it because of the time and effort his mother put into his care and making sure he got all the therapy he needed."

"It took a *lot* of time," Mary Jane says, not even trying to describe or itemize the hundreds and hundreds of visits to doctors, to clinics, to therapy sessions. What she *does* say is that, "As soon as possible, we got Andy started on speech therapy and lip reading. Andy reads lips fantastically, mainly because he started so early. The teachers he had were adamantly against signing and made him learn how to speak. Eric and Andy were always able to communicate. I think the reason Eric developed his sensitivities toward people was because he got dragged everywhere. When I had to take Andy for therapy, Eric had to come along. And he'd also go with me to visit my mother in a nursing home after she became an invalid. After he had spent time visiting with my mother, Eric would visit with the other woman in the room."

"Andy's situation brought me to the realization that we are in the Lord's hands," Howard says. "I think this was when we really knew we needed something other than ourselves."

"Neither of us came from a religious background, but we felt it was important for us to get involved in a good church for the sake of the children," Mary Jane adds. "We just felt that had to be an important part of our lives. We felt Andy had to be taught about God's Word and that he had to be taught right. I think one reason Eric was not as well known at the church as some of the other youngsters was because Howard and I were older than most parents of fifteen-year-olds. [When the crash took place, Mary Jane was fifty-two and Howard was fifty-three.]"

"Andy went to Bridgeport University in Connecticut and graduated cum laude from the engineering school," Howard says. "We always tried to provide a constructive substitute for Eric, who knew there were certain things we did not want him doing and who knew there were certain groups of youngsters we did not want him to get involved with. Some of those youngsters shot off fireworks. That's illegal. So I would say to Eric, 'Let's go out and do something else' and we would always find something to do. We tried to establish our position in such a way that he would see that we understood his situation and that we wanted to help him. He never rode the minibike without asking for permission to ride it. The understanding was that the minibike was *mine*. That way, when other kids asked to use it, he could honestly say that *he* couldn't allow that because the minibike wasn't his."

Stoics? "No. No. I cannot be a stoic. I cry." So said Howard in the summer of 1980. "I suppose it's just that, by God's grace, we are strong," he added, knowing that the strength he and Mary Jane have displayed in public has been misinterpreted by some. "I feel that people in our situation become extremely sensitive because of their grief and they sometimes try to evaluate how other people are assessing their grief. From a thoroughly logical standpoint, how much or how little anyone appreciates my grief will do nothing to change what I am grieving about. Therefore, why should I get upset about what other people think about me? This is merely looking at it from a purely logical view and I am not going to say that this is the way I have always felt about this situation. But, given time and circumstances and a chance to think things through, this is the way I now see it. I can understand why some people looked at us and thought we were calloused. If you *look* like you are handling things well, it's logical for people to assume you *are* handling things well, that there is no grief. One thing that has been very important to me is the awareness that you cannot categorize individual grief and come up with an itemized laundry list. That's because each of us is different. At the start of your grief, it's like a bottomless pit. You have to go back to the Scriptures where it tells us, 'Lean not unto thine own understanding.' We just can't understand grief. All we can do is lean on the Lord and ask Him to get us through it."

The strength of the Borlozes was there from the outset of their ordeal, perhaps to an extraordinary degree because they had over the years learned how to contend with the pain that had been visited upon them as they gave so much of themselves, their time, their money, their lives to help Andy. When one must constantly give of oneself, it can break or strengthen the will, the spirit. The Borlozes did not break. Their strength, built on inner resolve and the knowledge that God could be depended upon, enabled them to almost always keep their emotions in check when in public. Thus, to outsiders, it seemed that rearing Andy was not much different than bringing up any other boy.

Years of steeling their emotions when in public enabled the Borlozes to do the same after Eric had died. It was the time honored stiff-upper-lip routine, which is admired by a few people and misread by many more. What goes unnoticed is that, while the upper lip may be stiff, the lower one is trembling. No one except Andy saw Howard and Mary Jane wrapped in each other's arms as their tears mingled when he brought her the news about Eric in the early hours of Sunday, November 12, 1978. Who was there to see Mary Jane that day in January 1982 as she sat through more than three hours of interviewing, her head tilted slightly forward much of the time, apparently so in control—until the tears she had strained to keep back began leaking from the reservoir they had formed when they fell on the inside of her eyeglasses? Who was there when Howard got up, walked into the kitchen of his house, honked his considerable nose, and explained, "When I'm upset, I have to keep moving"? Who was there to hear Mary Jane say, "You want to forget—but you don't want to forget Eric. How do you do that? He was so special"? Who heard Howard when he said less than a year after the accident, "If I were without Christ, I'd have been gas-pipe material. Knowing that someday I'll be walking with Eric in heaven is very important to me"?

"We've tried not to create any shrines to Eric's memory," Mary Jane says. "He's with the Lord and so are the other kids, and that's comforting." Although she continually expected that at any moment she would be freed from her anguish, Mary Jane found that her todays were as painful as her yesterdays and that the hope she stored up in her tomorrows faded into disappointment when those days were added to her calendar of sorrows.

"When I try to handle things by myself, that's when it's the hardest," Mary Jane says. "As soon as I put things in God's hands, I seem to be able to manage better. As much as some people have helped—and some of them were marvelous—it still comes down to the fact that you have to face your grief alone and that the only lasting help comes from the Lord. And yet there are days when I can't believe all the things that have happened to us and that there really is a God. Then I think, 'That's a ridiculous thought. I *know* God exists and I know that He's the only source of lasting comfort. I read one book by a mother who had lost a teenage son in an accident. She was a Christian and she made it sound so easy how she got over her grief. I just couldn't accept that. Some thoughts kept coming back and there were times when I'd just say, 'Lord, I don't understand. I just *can't* understand.' As a born-again Christian, I believe so totally in the Lord and yet there have been those bad times. I had to sit myself down and really think things through. Each time I did, I came back to the same answers—only the Lord knows how it all fits together and only He can help me."

Mary Jane Borloz apparently came to a poignant moment in her struggle the day she asked two questions. The first question: "Why *me*?" That was followed momentarily by the second question: "Why *not* me?"

Early in 1982, Mary Jane said, "If anyone had told me three years ago that I'd still be grieving, I would have said that person was crazy. This third year was the worst for me. Just the other day, I said to Howard, 'I've got to let go of the memories.' You have to go on with your lives. It's easy to say. I'm just having a hard time with it. I can't help if I believe that Eric was special. I miss him."

"Every day with your children is precious," Howard said that day. "The trouble is, you don't miss the water until the well is dry. There is a vast abyss between logic and emotions. Where we draw the line, I confess I do not know. I cry and then the tears stop. Then I discover that a sea of tears changes nothing."

Howard is seated at the head of a table in the family room of the house he built. His forearms rest on the arms of the chair, the fingers of both hands knitted together and resting almost in his lap. Howard's words tumble out a little slower than usual, as if they are making a long journey from the depths of his being. That, upon reflection, may be precisely where they came from. Howard went on to say, "Without my faith in God, I would have been a basket case. My faith is my foundation. We have been to groups that try to help the grieving. I've read books about the subject. I've listened to psychologists and other people lecture on the topic. All I can say after all I've heard and read is that God has made each of us separate and distinct people and that no answer or set of answers will satisfy the needs of everyone. I seem to be most vulnerable when we're singing a hymn in church. The feelings and the tears are fleeting, but they are definitely real. If someone's standing next to me at a time like that, that person might think, 'What's his problem?' There are times when, without provocation, I can see five caskets lined up in front of the church. But for the most part, the memories draw me closer, not away." One of the surest memory-rousers is a photograph of Eric that Howard keeps in his wallet. Howard pulled out the badly worn picture one afternoon, looked at it and, with genuine concern, asked: "What do I do when it gets too frayed?"

14

Martha and Larry Carroll

During summers in the mid-1940s, Larry Carroll would drive to the home of his girlfriend, Martha Miles Scranton, and then head for the Jersey shore and a day at the ocean. That was back in the days when Larry drove a seven-passenger Chrysler Imperial. The auto was dubbed "The Ark," in deference to its size. Larry remembers those days with fondness. "We also used to go to dances, ice skating parties, and to quite a few art museums because of Martha's interest in art," Larry says. "She was studying to be a fine arts teacher. There was another thing—wherever we went, Martha was always the prettiest girl in the group."

Martha, who was born and reared in Jersey City, dated Larry throughout the four years she went to the New Jersey Teachers College, which was then located in Newark. They had met at the Summit Avenue Baptist Church in Jersey City. Larry's father, who sang professionally, was the choir director at the church. Grandfather Carroll had been a minister in the Reformed Church of America until he was somehow killed by a railroad train in 1899 in Jersey City. Martha's father was a chemist, who she says, "made materials for batteries. Whenever I got a call from a company like Eveready, I had to be sure to write down all the information very carefully." Her mother died of cancer when Martha, who has a twin sister, was twelve.

"When I was eighteen, I had a full-time job, went to the New York University business school, and was courting my wife-to-be," Larry says. "That is the kind of energy that's reserved for the young." In 1942, after Larry had enlisted in the navy, he and Martha were married. Following the war, they and Larry, Jr. moved to Harrington Park, New Jersey, which is just down the road from Westwood. Larry then set about trying to earn a living as a singer.

"Most of the time I was in quartets that sang at state fairs," Larry recalls. "After I had traveled with a water show that went halfway around the country, I decided that that was no way to live. My sister Libby was working for a man who had an upholstery business in Westwood. Her boss wanted to sell his business. I told him, 'No thanks.' But then I wound up buying the business." The Carrolls moved to Westwood and had four more children—Alan, Leslie, Bill and Thomas. "To supplement my income from the store, I got a job singing at the Presbyterian church in Tenafly," Larry says.

There is one main difference between the Carrolls: Martha speaks sparingly; Larry was last at a loss for words in about 1938. "I'm so quiet that people ignore me," Martha says with a tinge of regret that can be detected in her soft, small voice. "I taught for only a short time, but I've always thought I'd like to go back to the classroom. I don't know if I could take it, though. In 1975, I was hospitalized with a heart problem. Valve trouble. I'm still on medication and I have to be careful."

In February 1982, Martha had this to say about her grieving: "It's calmed down, but once in a while it gets to me and puts me in the depths. It's encouraging to think that Thomas is in heaven and that I'll be seeing him there someday.

"Before they moved away, the McCarthys were a big help. Jan would come to the store, sit down and talk with me for an hour or more. Nedaleine Biscaye was also a big help. It meant a lot to be able to talk things out with people. Once in a while I'll find something that reminds me of Thomas and it will get to me. One day, I was in the kitchen looking at a recipe card. On the back of it I found a note that Thomas had written there in his quick scribble. It said, 'Mom, I'm at the concert in the park.' That got to me."

Tommy's death was not the only thing the Carrolls had to cope with. Six weeks after the accident, Larry's ninety-five-year-old mother died. Even before that the Carrolls had known that Larry was suffering from a problem that was becoming more and more serious. The first indication that something was amiss came in early 1975 when Larry developed double vision. An ophthalmologist checked him out, found nothing wrong, and suggested that Larry go to a neurologist. Despite a variety of examinations and X rays, the neurologist was unable to track down the problem. Larry preferred to forget about the matter, but gradually there were other symptoms he could not be so blithe about because they were apparent not only to him but to those around him. One of those manifestations was what seemed to be a bit of paralysis on his left side. Larry also began having so much trouble with his balance that when he visited the Hayhursts, David would help him down the steps of the front porch and then down the cement steps that led to the driveway.

"My left arm also wasn't working properly," Larry says. "My left foot didn't want to pick up. My speech became slurred. The doctor suspected I'd had a stroke. In September '78, Thomas was helping me carry a boxspring out of the basement of the store. At the top of the stairs was a *large* fire extinguisher. The box spring hit it and knocked it loose. As it started to fall, I was afraid it might land on Thomas, who was below me. I deliberately pushed my left hip out to the side so the fire extinguisher would hit me and be deflected away from Thomas. It still hurts me where it hit [this was in late March 1980], but nothing was broken. That injury just made it more difficult for the doctor to figure out exactly what my trouble was. A therapist at the hospital said to me, 'You don't act like someone who's had a stroke.' He suggested that I go to another doctor. So I went to a neurologist in Westwood. By that time, I didn't like being in the store because my speech was so slurred that it was embarrassing. I also didn't have anyone to help me until Martha came down to the store. I was so tired that the first thing I'd do when I got to the store was go to sleep. My favorite place was on a big sofa bed. It had wings on it and I'd just get in one of those corners of that thing, get wedged in, and go to sleep. I was also having problems with my left hand, which became so drawn up that it almost looked like a claw.

"When I went to the doctor, he sent me to have a CAT scan done. [CAT scan—computerized axial tomography—is an exotic X-ray process in which incredibly thin "slices" of the anatomy can be magnified greatly and studied on a video screen.] They found I had a tumor on the right side of my brain. On February 28, 1979, I was operated on at Pascack Valley Hospital in Westwood. Dr. George Jacobs, a neurosurgeon, performed the surgery, which lasted from about seven or seven-thirty in the morning until about two or three in the afternoon."

The night before the operation, Reverend Wortman was at the Carrolls' house for a time of prayer. He was also at the hospital the next morning and, while the surgery was performed, spent the time in prayer in the hospital chapel. Those prayers, as well as the ones offered by other people, were answered. It was learned later that, according to Martha, "They lost Larry on the operating table but were able to bring him back." Neither he nor Martha elaborated on the operation, which was a massive craniotomy in which a large section of the right side of the skull had to be removed. Most of the tumor was removed, but a portion could not be reached. For twelve days, Larry was in the intensive care unit.

Many people prayed for Larry, who was widely known and respected in Christian circles in northeastern New Jersey. As Jan McCarthy expressed it in the summer of '79, "This was a modern-day Job. He had lost his son, his mother, and his health all in a few months. We were so close to Larry because we had rented our store from him and because he was one of the men who discipled us when Bob and I first came to know the Lord. His life reflected his belief in Christ. Until just a few weeks ago, even to those who had a strong faith, it seemed he would never survive. We saw him in the hospital and he looked so pathetic. It wasn't the Larry we had known. So people began getting together to pray for him. After all of us started praying, Larry got worse—much worse—before he began to come back. When he was at his worst, I think God was calling for all of us to act with our faith and not according to what our eyes saw. Our eyes saw that there was no hope, but the last time I saw Larry in the hospital two weeks ago, he was the *old* Larry we used to know. Although he could barely talk, Larry was quoting Scriptures. The doctor says there will have to be a second operation to get the rest of the tumor. But all of us are praying that this won't be necessary."

Larry Carroll's remarkable recuperation continued. So did the prayers of many who knew him or knew of him. He had been transferred on April 16th to the New Jersey Rehabilitation Center in East Orange. During his days there, Larry did what he had done in so many other places: He quoted Bible verses to anyone who would listen. Among those who listened was a nurse who asked him, "Have you memorized the *whole* Bible?" No, Larry hadn't accomplished that, but he had committed enough of it to memory that he was able to draw upon its strength and its promises to carry him through those fearful days.

On June 25, Larry returned home for the first time for a brief visit. "That was like resurrection day," he said later of that glorious event. He was able to get around only in a wheelchair then and a few times during the next couple of months he made it to church with Martha. Then came the most memorable day of all: August 24. That was the day Larry made it home for keeps. "They thought I'd have to use a wheelchair for the rest of my life, but when I came home that day all I had to use was a quad cane," Larry pointed out a few months later. At that time he was still terribly weak, was wobbly on his feet, and looked sallow. Other than that, he was fine, his enthusiasm for life was returning and he had regained much of the weight he had lost after having fallen from one hundred and sixty pounds to one twenty-two.

"I'm here because the Lord didn't feel it was my time to go at the age of fifty-nine," he said after taking his pills. "It was also His will that Thomas should join Him at the age of fourteen. Others didn't expect me to make it. I expected to. 'We love him because he first loved us.' First John tells us that marvelous truth. God does something and we respond, but unless we have a new birth and a spiritually renewed mind we aren't going to be able to see the promises of God and we won't be able to understand that all He has said is the truth. People have to be born again because the natural man doesn't understand the things of God. First Corinthians 2:9 and 10 tells us, 'Eye hath not seen, nor ear heard, neither have entered into the heart of man, the things which God hath prepared for them that love him. But God hath revealed them unto us by His Spirit. . . .'

"Quite a few people who were ill when I was in the hospital didn't make it back to health. When we were at the hospital after the CAT scan, it was found that there were problems with the blood vessels in my head. The doctor said an angiogram was needed to help determine exactly what was wrong. He asked us to read a form explaining the dangers of the angiogram and to sign it only if we were willing to go ahead with it. The form indicated that there was some danger involved and that blindness, paralysis, and even death could result. 'Should we sign this?' Martha said. 'Yes,' I told her. 'Commitment is the key. We have committed ourselves to this doctor. What's even more important is that my commitment to Christ is complete.'

"After I spoke with Barbara Hayhurst on the phone on the night of the accident, I prayed, 'Father, I commit myself to thee to live this night by the facts found in your Word and not to live by my feelings.' When I heard about Thomas, it felt like I had been kicked by a mule. We were able to overcome the pain only because God gave us the strength not to be ruled by our emotions.

"One of the things that helped me the most was the realization that God *is* in control. We, as humans, are inclined to feel that when things don't go the way we'd like them to go that they are out of control and that God has *not* been watching over us. We may even feel that He has turned His back on us. Over the years, as the result of study and seeing God at work, I've learned that He is *never* unaware of my needs. So, when my child was riding in that van that night, it was a great comfort to know that God's eyes were on Thomas. One of my favorite verses concerning this is Second Chronicles 16:9: 'For the eyes of the Lord run to and fro throughout the whole earth, to show Himself strong in the behalf of them whose heart is perfect toward Him.' No hearts can be more perfect than those in which Christ lives. So I *know* God was watching 'to show Himself strong' at the moment that Thomas ended this physical life.

"Scripture tells us to not look at the past with regret, but to 'press toward the mark for the prize of the high calling of God in Christ Jesus.' All things work together for good for those who love God. Do you love God? From the bad things of our past and from the trouble we have gone through, God molds the fiber that makes each of us usable. If you look back and *don't* love God, it can crush you. We have to challenge others about their faith and we have to challenge ourselves about it, too. It's like when I was talking with an eighty-year-old man who wanted to discuss spiritual matters. 'I'm not a sinner,' he said. 'George,' I said, 'those words come from your mouth and make it evident that you *are* a sinner. What you said about not being a sinner is a sin in itself.' Then George said, 'Does God say I'm a sinner?' I told him, 'Indeed He does. He tells us in His word that, "All have sinned and come short of the glory of God." And *you* say, 'No, God. Not George.' This man saw that he was calling God a liar. People have to see that we are, by our very humanity, sinful and that God will lift us out of sin and give us a new life through His Son. To be born again is an act of faith, a commitment that changes people's lives as nothing else can.

"God took care of me in many ways during my illness. I had wanted to drop our health insurance because it covered very little of the expenses connected with Martha's heart problem. But Martha asked me to keep it. We did. My medical bills came to $60,000. A large part of that was taken care of by the insurance. It was just another case of God proving that He *does* know our situations and our needs, and that He *does* provide for us."

If Larry Carroll seems to come across with uncommon and forceful spiritual drive, well, that's precisely the way he is. He can, and often does, launch into what amounts to sermonettes at the mention of many topics. One of his chief concerns has been for the spiritual well being of people with whom he comes into contact. This was true even while at work.

"I always used the store as a place of witness," Larry says. "For fourteen years we had prayer meetings in the back of the store. After Bob McCarthy took over the place, he carried it on among some of the businessmen in the area. I used to have spiritual adventures in the store. Right across the street from my place was a liquor store. Above it were apartments. One of those apartments had ripped shades. It was well known as a house of ill repute and also as a place for drug dealing. From the store, I was able to look up to that apartment and sometimes see a boy who looked about twelve years old. He would sometimes be at the window playing with a cat. I began praying for that boy, that the Lord would somehow save him. Bob McCarthy and I agreed to pray for that boy's salvation. Well, that youngster finally came to a Bible study and he received the Lord as his Savior. Then he began coming to our church and now he's going to be a missionary."

You may be of the opinion that the depth and consistency of Larry's Christian life came easily and that it merely sprang forth from the backgrounds of him and his family. After all, his grandfather had been a minister. You might assume that he was a strong Christian not long after he was out of diapers. But Larry explains:

"Shortly after getting into the upholstery business I found out I was allergic to cotton. That was bad because I was constantly using cotton. I beat myself frantic trying to figure a way out of the mess. My allergy got me so discouraged that I told my wife I didn't think life was worth living. 'What's the sense of life, anyhow?' I said to her. During this period we were taking Larry, Jr., to Sunday School at the Reformed church in Westwood. I decided to stay for the men's class and I saw these people at the church with joy in their lives. And everyone I talked with there had a testimony about how they were born-again Christians. Jack Young, Sr., took me to a Christian Businessmen's luncheon. There I saw and heard the same things that I'd found in the men's class at the church. These were happy people who testified that Jesus Christ was their personal Savior. At that time I was a member of a choir in a church a few miles away in Tenafly. I liked the choir there, but I preferred the Sunday School at the Westwood church. When I got to the Tenafly church for choir rehearsal one day, I pulled into the parking lot there and just sat there thinking. I had just been reading the fifth chapter of Second Corinthians that, 'If any man be in Christ, he is a new creature.' I knew I was about as far from the Lord as I could get and I said to myself, 'New creature? That's not me. I'd sorta like to be a new creature, though.' And then I prayed, 'Lord Jesus, would You please come into my life and make me a new creature?' Right there, right in that parking lot, I started to become a new creature. God began to take charge of my life.

"Many people know *about* God. Shakespeare knew the Bible, but he didn't know God. Sad. It doesn't matter if you know *about* God. You have to know *Him*. To surrender your life to God is the beginning of the excitement of Christian living. When I came to know something of the power of God, I told Him, 'Father, I'm ready to do as You've told me to do in Your Word. Please fill me with Your Spirit and use me.' That very night I spoke with a man who was a Sunday School superintendent and I found he had never accepted Christ into his heart. I asked him to pray with me and, to my surprise, he invited Christ into his life. That's how it all started for me and that's why I'm so enthusiastic about the things of God.

"But just because you're spiritually in control, don't think your emotions can't get going and take over. When I returned home for good from the rehabilitation center, I saw the picture of Thomas in the living room. Satan reminded me of a couple times during the last year of Thomas' life that I had done things that had made him miserable. Immediately, the devil got me started on a guilt trip. I got so low I didn't think I could get up again. The devil suggested to me, 'What a rat you were.' We have to be careful about guilt. It can be destructive. We must keep in mind that God has forgiven us and that all those things in the past are taken care of. To still feel guilty is to not believe that God has promised us forgiveness. We have to accept power from God to overcome the calamities of life. Whenever a defeat comes along for me, I have to be very careful because depression is *right behind it*. That's my natural way. But God's grace is sufficient. His strength is made perfect in our weakness. When I walk into the living room these days and see the picture of Thomas, I sometimes say, 'Hi. How're things going?'"

A few weeks after his return home, Larry volunteered to be a counselor for the "700 Club" Christian television show. Ever since then he has made weekly visits to the office in Allendale where local calls to the show are funneled. He has given Christian advice to hundreds of callers, including fifteen women whose young children have died. Larry also launched into another ministry, a by-product of the lengthy walks he takes around Westwood to get the exercise he needs so much. Larry, ever the conversationalist, chats with people on the sidewalks, in stores, at red lights, and wherever he stops for a cup of coffee.

Men, women, children, sales clerks, policemen, waitresses—anyone Larry encounters—all hear one form or another of the love and power of God. Just about everybody in Westwood knows Larry and more than a few people have marveled at his strength both as a man and as a Christian.

"A year and a half after my surgery I had a CAT scan that revealed there was no more tumor. People had been praying for me and I *knew* there would be no need for that second operation."

What about Martha? It is obvious that Martha can be, as she indicated, ignored. Surely, though, the Lord has kept tabs on her. So, as best he can, has Larry, Jr. His father's strength is manifested in many ways and is acknowledged by many. What about his mother, quiet Martha? Says Larry Carroll, Jr.: "I can honestly say that I *never*—can I really say that?—yes, I *never* saw her crumble under it all. And that has included a lot—from Thomas' death to my father's illness, surgery, and recuperation." Quiet Martha. Her deeds do the speaking for her.

15

Connie and Walt Van Beers

Connie's first glimpse of Walt was when she saw a picture of him in his marine uniform. As far as she was concerned, he passed inspection, so to speak. At that moment, Connie was in Walt's house, where she had come with her sister Trudy, who was dating his brother Bill. When Walt, no longer a marine, came home a few minutes later, he met Connie and briefly chatted with her before she had to leave. As she was pulling out of the driveway, Bill ran out of the house. "He asked me if I wanted to go out with his brother," Connie recalls. "I said, 'If he wants a date, let him call me on the phone.' " Walt called. After the first date, he called again and again. But after fifteen months of phoning, Walt stopped calling for dates; he didn't have to because by then he and Connie were man and wife.

Connie, who was born in Den Haag (The Hague), Holland, came to the U.S. in June 1959 with her parents and two sisters. Walt grew up in Midland Park, New Jersey. After his tour of duty with the marines, he went to work for his brother Ed in the paint business.

"Then I went to work for a loan business for about eight-and-a-half years," Walt says. "I didn't enjoy that because I was involved with people who were not able to pay their bills and I wound up having to repossess their cars and assign their wages. That became very distasteful to me. Some of the people were really down and out, and it bothered me to see the situations they were in. I decided I wanted to get a college degree. I wanted the education itself and I wanted to end up being a teacher. A friend I had known for years owned a paint store and he asked me to go into business with him. I did. I also went to William Paterson College [in Wayne, New Jersey]. It took eight years of going at night, but I finally got my B.A. degree. I was thirty-four years old at the time. I majored in sociology and had a minor in psychology. The reason I got into those areas was because I've always been deeply interested in what motivates people, what makes them do the good things they do and what makes others continue in their evil ways. I never found the answers in college. I also gave up my plan of teaching because I knew I wouldn't make the kind of money I was making in the paint business. The business has kept on expanding and we've opened up a couple other places."

"My partner, George Gorter, invited us to attend a Bible study he went to. I was interested because my search for meaning and for God had started when I was about the age of 10 or 11 because there was a lot of turmoil in my life when I was young. What I found out as we got into the studies was that I was hungry to learn more about the things that were being taught. These studies were teaching me things I had never known anything about. These were things right out of the Bible, things that pertained to me and to my family and about how God wants us to live.

"If you are not in God's Word, how are you going to know what He has to tell you? God has something to say to every one of us. The only places I found complete answers about the meanings of life were in the Bible studies and at the Pascack church when Pastor Fred preached. We felt at home in that church and we became members there."

All of this took time. One event that speeded up the process took place in October of 1975 when, at the urging of a friend, Walt, Connie, Maria, and Donna spent a weekend at the Word of Life camp in up-state New York. There the Van Beerses were deeply stirred by a message by Harry Bollback of the Word of Life staff.

"What he was saying was that God was asking everyone to put away all the things that were restricting them from accepting Him the way a little child would," Walt points out. "After hearing him, I decided that, for once in my life, I was going to trust God and try to believe Him and follow Him. I felt it was time to let all the barriers down, to stop making excuses. Then Bollback gave a call for people to raise their hands if they wanted Christ in their lives. None of us knew what the others were doing because we had all been asked to bow our heads and close our eyes. What none of us knew when that invitation was given was that *all of us* had raised our hands—Connie, the girls, and me. After the speaker prayed, Connie and the girls started crying."

Before that evening was over, all the Van Beerses had been coun-seled about the decisions they had made, to be certain they understood what it meant to invite Christ into their lives. A man who spoke with Walt sensed that he was holding back. "I told him that, for the most part, I was willing to take this thing step by step but that there were a few areas I found hard to deal with," Walt says. "Overwhelming" is how Connie sums up the experience.

It was in 1975 that Christ entered their lives. John entered their lives via adoption. "John is a full-blooded Korean," Connie says. "When we got him through the Welcome House in Doylestown, Pennsylvania, he was eighteen months old and was suffering from malnutrition. For two weeks he didn't smile and for two months he couldn't keep food down. But he's been a joy in our lives."

The pieces in life's puzzle were starting to fit together. Connie, who *"knew* there was a God *somewhere,"* found He was not an unknowable "it." Walt had completed his education, was doing well in business and was having many of his questions about life and Christianity answered. There would always be more questions, for he had a probing mind. Then came the accident—and a whole new set of questions.

While driving his car Walt would keep the windows up so no one could hear him scream at God. On other days there was no anger. The emptiness Walt felt, though, was no relief. Those were the times when, while driving, Walt thought he should just aim for a tree and end it all. But he didn't because he realized this was a cop-out on the rest of the family.

"We had thought Connie would be the basket case," Flo Cussimanio says. "I think it was on the Monday after the accident that we went to the funeral home with Walt and Connie to take care of some details there. We offered to drive, but Walt said, 'No, I have to lick this thing. *I* have to drive.' He seemed so strong then. After three, four months it was obvious he hadn't licked it and a lot of us were thinking, 'Come on, Walt, get it together.' We didn't understand. We let him down."

"Before the accident, I had been playing tennis with Walt early on Wednesday mornings," Tom Cussimanio says. "After we played we'd shower, have breakfast and head to work. Then came the accident. Walt obviously didn't feel like playing tennis for awhile. Two months after the accident I asked him, 'Do you want to play?' He said, 'Yeah.' But you could tell his heart was not in it. I asked him if we should stop for a while again. He said, 'Yes.' It's been three years since then and we've never played again. Walt let it be known there wasn't much anyone could do to help him. I withdrew. That's what he seemed to be saying he wanted. Both Walt and Connie later said that we should have been stronger. Walt said he didn't understand why people hadn't been more outward in trying to help, but he also admitted he had expressed a desire to be left alone."

During the summer after the accident, Walt said, "On the one hand, I knew that this thing had happened, but there was another part of me that kept saying, 'No.' The period right after the accident was strengthening because so many people were around or were doing things to let you know they were reaching out to try to help. You'd open the front door of the house and there would be things that people had brought—pies, cookies, all sorts of things. Then everyone leaves you alone and reality hits. On the way home from work I would tell myself that when I got home Maria would be there. But when I'd sit down at the dinner table, her seat would always be empty. I had always trusted that when Maria was out at night that she would be all right. After the accident I had a sense of failure, a feeling that I had let this child get away from me, that I wasn't able to protect her and that I should have been able to. Those things are not true, I now know. It's all in the Lord's timing. You come full cycle and realize, as a friend told me, 'All you are trying to determine is when we should die, and that's something only God can take care of.'

"We're in a church where, Sunday by Sunday, people share their problems. People who have cancer. People who are facing critical surgery. People who have lost a parent or who are going blind. I remember praying with and for people in the congregation who had such problems. But you never feel that anything of such magnitude could happen to *you.* Somehow, there seems to be within each of us—at least it's within me, I know—a feeling that those things always happen to the other person. Now I know that's not true. At first, I was bitter about it. If anybody could have turned his back on God, I feel it would have been me. One of the things that helped me most in my healing was when Don [Hayhurst] said, 'There's a reason for the accident and time will give us the answers.' I kept saying to myself, 'How could he believe that?' But I knew he was right and I drew strength from that."

When the accident took place, Connie was thirty-nine years old and Walt forty. They were the youngest of the four couples and were also still fairly young in their faith. Both were and still are active and energetic people. Despite their similarities in some areas, they grieved in different ways. The routes they took can be seen in these lengthy quotes from Connie and Walt in late November 1981 and mid-February 1982:

"The first Christmas [after the accident] was awful," Connie began. "We were all in such shock that you really couldn't call it Christmas at all. I feel that 1979, after the reality had set in that we had lost Maria, was the worst year for me. It was also terrible for Walter. I had thought we would grieve together, but that did not happen. We grieved individually. He went upstairs after supper *every night* and read or listened to tapes on Revelation and the 'end times,' plus many, many other books on death and the afterlife until becoming exhausted or falling asleep. I would get the kids off to bed and then I would sit here in our den. Many nights I would sit and cry and cry, and say to myself, 'I have nobody.' I felt like the loneliest person in the world and I think the Lord taught me through this that I *had* to rely on Him. That is the only way I got through it.

"A lot of people in the church thought we were getting a lot of support and help from the body itself, but I did not feel that way. I felt there was much more that people could have done, like come over and have coffee or just come and chat. I would get phone calls once in a while, but I expected more, to be honest. Later I understood that if you have not gone through this kind of thing that you do not know what the person who did is struggling with. Even Fred [Pastor Beveridge] did not understand it all. He tried so hard and was great in many ways, but even he did not understand what it's like. There was a pain in my heart *all the time.* This is what people do not understand— the inner feelings. They can't. People later said they wanted to ask us how we were doing, but they didn't want to bring up the subject. They didn't know that we *wanted* them to bring it up. By not saying anything, it made us think that they had forgotten us. I would have reacted the same way, though, if I had not had a child who had been in that accident.

"During 1979 Walter and I, who love each other, were emotionally drained and had difficulty relating to one another. Statistics say that seventy per cent of the married couples who lose a child wind up divorced. I understand why. I thought at times we were not going to make it.

"In September of '79, I went on a retreat. They had all kinds of workshops you could attend there. One was for women with husbands who were unsaved. Another was for divorced women. There was one that dealt with grief. Barbara Hayhurst had gone on this trip and we went to the workshop on grief. The woman in charge had lost a seven-year-old daughter to leukemia and now she was explaining what her grieving had been like. I began to sob uncontrollably. Then women started singing "For Those Tears I Died." Nobody there except Barbara and I knew that that had been Maria's favorite song. I was crying and shaking from top to bottom. I felt as if I was being choked. And then all of a sudden it was like the yoke fell off and I had total relief. It was *absolutely amazing.* After that, things started to get better for me. I shared this experience with Walter. I have to be honest . . . I don't want to hurt Walter . . . but for months he kept saying, 'I lost her. I lost her.' I said, 'What about me? I lost her, too.' He said, 'Yes, I know.' But still in his own mind he was so wrapped up with his own grief that he was not thinking about what I was going through. From November, when the accident happened, until the next September, all I did was try to get Walter over his grieving. I had said I was going to get him out of his grief, not deal with my own. But there was no communication. He would just go upstairs.

"I also had Donna and John to take care of. I feel very sure the Lord gave John to us at the time He did because He knew what was going to happen to us. He gave us a child who is very loving and kind and good-natured. I leaned on John more than I did on anyone in the family. I wanted to lean on Donna, but I had to remember she was hurting, too. John knew Maria had died, but he was too young to understand much about it. I told him Maria's body was in a cemetery but that her soul was with Jesus in heaven because she had given her life to Him. One day, I took John with me when I went to Maria's grave. We bought some flowers and walked over to the grave. I started crying, sort of half praying and crying at the same time. John put his hand on my shoulder and said, 'It's OK, Mommy. You can cry. It's OK.' It was just beautiful. One day about a year and a half after the accident, we were coming home from church after an evening service and John called out, 'Ria.' He called her that instead of Maria. John asked where she was. I said she was in heaven. 'Well, isn't she going to go to bed?' John asked. I told him I was sure she would be going to bed. Then he said, 'I wonder if Ria has her pajamas up there.' "

"I was not able to help Connie," Walt said. "That's true. My grieving was completely inward. My days consisted of going to work, coming home, eating dinner, saying only what had to be said and no more. When darkness came and I could close my eyes, I would thank God because the darkness was like a hiding place for me. Sometimes I felt I wanted to be in a closet with the door closed. My bouts of anger came quite frequently early on and lasted for about three months. What lasted longer were the verbal attacks I made on the Lord. I wanted badly to be dead. It took a long time before I realized Connie had been carrying a heavy load and that she was hanging on by a thread. I was finally able to see Connie had needs because I started to come along with my healing. After I got some of my hurts behind me and got my emotions under control, we decided we still had our lives to live. We also still had two children to think of.

"One of the first people who got through to me was Jack Young, Jr., who had lost his daughter to spinal meningitis," Walt pointed out. "Every once in a while he'd just pop into the store. One day he came in and asked me, 'How ya doin' today?' My immediate thought was that I'd just gloss over the question. But instead I said, 'Do you *really* wanna know?' He said he did, so I told Jack, 'As a matter of fact, I'm uptight, angry, and frustrated.' He smiled and said, 'I understand. Can I pray with you?' I said, 'Fine.' Later that day I realized he had been through the same feelings I was going through. His coming when he did was part of my healing. When he smiled and said he understood, it helped me realize he *did* understand. I think there were times when Pastor did not know what to say to me, but that was all right because there were people like him who ministered just by being around you or just by putting an arm around your shoulder. I remember John Hartman throwing his arms around me. It was supportive love and I needed it.

"One day about two years after the accident, I was angry and I was talking with Don Hayhurst. He said, 'Walt, I can't tell you what to do except that you've got to throw the whole situation at the feet of Jesus, really give it all to Him.' When I went to bed that night I said a different prayer for the first time since the accident. Before that night, it was almost always a prayer asking God, 'Why? Why? Why?' But that night I said, 'Lord, I do not know why, but I am going to accept it. I'm tired of banging this thing around. If this is really what You meant to have happen, then I will accept it.' That very night I had a vision that was so complete and so powerful that I have really never questioned God again. I had this vision of a being that put one hand on each of my shoulders. He was directly in front of me and said, 'I am in control. Trust me.' I responded by saying something I have never said to anyone. I said, 'Yes, Master.'

"The second part of the vision was off in the distance. There were people climbing a hill and there was a man in a robe leading them and there was a great deal of light behind him. I could not make out who he was. Off to my right—and you must remember that my wife was sleeping through all this—there was a little girl dancing. The girl was not Maria. She was like a cartoon figure. How did I know this was a vision and not a dream? It was not a dream because what I saw stayed in front of me for about five minutes. I was wide awake and was looking at these things in front of me. I was totally awake and stayed that way for a good two hours. I think the incident helped me quite a bit."

"Sometimes when I think about the accident I still get teary-eyed, but it doesn't last too long any more," Connie said. "One nice thing to find out about was the letters that Maria and David Hayhurst wrote to each other while he was at college. In one letter she told David about an argument she had had with me. In her next letter she wrote him, 'I have taken your advice and talked it all out with my mother and everything is fine now.' It turned out that David was very beneficial to her spiritual growth. Another nice thing was that so many people wanted pictures of Maria. It was nice to know that Maria was not forgotten by people."

"One of the things that surprised me after the accident was that I found out that a lot of other people had suffered a lot of grief, too," Walt said. "We got letters from people we didn't even know and they told us about the tragedies in their lives. Some of those people were Christians and they used those letters as a witness to us about how God would carry us through.

"Psalm 139 became my favorite. It talks about how God knows the beginning and the end. Every one of us will have to die. If Jesus is not the bottom line for us, we are lost. When I understood that and the fact that it's *God's* timetable that counts, that's when my anger went away. Unless someone can tell the exact moment he or she is going to die, then it means they are not in control and that God is. I *know* God is in control.

"It's taken more than three years, but now the actual healing as a family has started. We've been trying to understand where each member in the family has been in their grieving process and it's been beneficial. It may seem odd, but just looking at Connie's toes sometimes makes me think of Maria. Toes are ugly things. They're bent out of shape. They stick out in all directions. But *my wife* has beautiful toes. The day Maria took charge of the sailboat I couldn't handle, I noticed her toes. They were just like Connie's. To myself I said, 'Maria, you've got beautiful toes.' "

Walt wandered a circuitous and tortuous route before conquering his grief. Among those who were aware that he had done so was Donna. Early in 1982, Donna spoke about how her father had grieved for so long and about how her parents had, at long last, united their efforts to win the battle. "Now they're like honeymooners," she said.

Another step in Walt's recovery came in the fall of 1981, when Walt was getting ready to drive to work. He placed his briefcase on top of his car while he took care of something. Then he got in the car and drove off. When he realized his briefcase was missing, Walt remembered placing it on the car roof. He drove back along the route he had just come, eyes peering everywhere for the briefcase, which among other items contained "a large amount of money." Connie joined the search. So did the police. They never found the briefcase.

"For two days I was really upset with myself," Walt admits. "Then I decided I couldn't go on like that. Being angry with myself wasn't going to bring the briefcase or the money back, and it was going to do me a lot of harm. A little while after I reached that conclusion, I had another thought. I realized I had forgiven myself, even though it hadn't been easy. I also realized I had never completely forgiven the men in the other van. I knew nothing about them except that they had been hard workers. Then I thought about Jesus on the cross when He said, 'Forgive them, for they know not what they do.' I also remembered that the Bible tells us to forgive seventy times seven, which is something Don had told us about when he urged all of us to go to the memorial service for the two men. When I realized all those things, I completely forgave those men and asked God to do the same. The anger I had felt toward them has gone and has not returned.

"Connie and I talked about how we had lost something more valuable than the money when we lost Maria. As hard and as frustrating as such trials are, there are reasons for them. It hurt to lose the money, but it was a loss that helped me take a very important step in my healing. The other day I prayed, 'Lord, I know You are teaching me lessons. I just hope I am learning because I can't take much more tutoring.' Forgiving those men made my healing complete. The bottom line is that we have to trust God in every circumstance, even though it is difficult to do this. I struggled, but I found out that God could take care of it all."

16

The Forgotten Ones

Grief has no favorites. As time passed after the accident, mourning gave way to sorrow. Then came grief. It is a cruel and insidious intruder that gnaws at minds and hearts. One of the most startling findings was that grief had entered the lives of many people. Everyone was aware that the eight parents grieved. Few saw that grief had other victims. Among them were those who were close to the families or who had youngsters of their own. These empathized with the eight parents to an extraordinary degree in some cases, and were at times tormented by memories and fears and by their inability to be of more comfort to the eight parents.

Nedaleine Biscaye, while sitting in her car at a red light one day during the summer after the crash, saw a boy on a bicycle who reminded her of Brian Hayhurst. The light changed. But while motorists behind her honked their horns, Nedaleine sat through the green, unable to drive on for a time because she had been overcome by tears. Grief takes many forms. Many of those variations have been experienced by people outside the immediate four families. That the grief of those on the periphery went almost completely unnoticed is not surprising. Grief wears many disguises and is often hard to detect. It also clouds the vision of those it grips. Even the grieving of the surviving brothers and sisters of the five who were still living at home went largely unrecognized for many months. The parents themselves had difficulty comprehending how much their surviving offspring were suffering—or that they were suffering at all. Now it is time to give some of these forgotten ones a chance to express what they have gone through.

"Right after the accident I went through a drastic change in personality," Donna Van Beers says. "I became outgoing! Prior to the accident I was a 'Mommy's girl.' My parents have talked with me about it. I guess I was trying to take my sister's place. I guess I felt I had to fill a gap. There was *constant* grief in our house and I didn't know how to handle it. My parents started giving me anything I wanted. A few days after the accident week we were shopping at Pathmark. I used to ask for magazines or junk food and my parents would always say, 'No.' This time, I wanted a couple magazines. My father said, 'Take whatever you want.' They bought me lots of clothes. They bought me *anything* I wanted. That helped for a while.

"Jennifer Knutzen, a good friend of mine, came to the house the day after the accident and spent the whole week with me. She skipped school and a few nights she slept in my room that week. I kinda floated through the first week. I remember Sunday afternoon—the day after the accident—that I was crying and my uncle came to my room and shook me and told me not to cry. Then my father came up, told my uncle to leave, and he hugged me and said, 'Cry if you have to. It's all right.' I cried.

"One thing I remember is that everything seemed to fit together just before the accident. Maria's birthday was coming up and I knew she liked a song by Anne Murray. It's called "You Needed Me." I bought it for my sister and I just felt I *had* to give it to her before her birthday. That's why, when she was in the kitchen getting the food ready to take to Randy that night, I put the record on and played that song for her. Then I played it again. She thought it was the radio at first, but after she heard the song a few times in a row she said, 'What's going on?' "

("The only thing I can remember is that Walter and I were grieving so much ourselves that we let Donna do what she wanted to do," Connie Van Beers points out. "We didn't see her crying. I didn't want to come right out and ask her why, but one day several months after the accident we were sitting on the couch and I asked her how she was taking it. She said, 'You don't see me cry because I'm doing my crying when I'm in bed.' ")

"At first, I just thought about having lost my brother," Bill Carroll says. "The next day, I realized I'd also lost my two best friends. It was a bummer. I wasn't forgotten by the people at church. I usually don't talk too much to them, but they were nice to me. Extra friendly. My brother and I didn't get along well. We were always fighting. But the last few weeks [before the accident], I can remember that for some reason we got along fine. He seemed to be getting stronger spiritually during that time and the last few weeks he was more enthusiastic about religion. For a while I was in a much more religious frame of mind. I tried not to sin as much, but after a while it faded. I got caught up at first in all the talk about how, 'They have been taken home.' Then it sank in: *They're dead* and I'm never going to see them again.

"To be honest, it would be better for me if my father wasn't so enthusiastic about his religion. Not a day—not an hour—goes by that he doesn't say something about religion, God, the Bible. Sometimes it can turn you off. But I *know* he's not making anything up. He's honest. It's just hard to be even close to being as enthusiastic about religion as he is. He's just too much. He doesn't think about anything else."

"At the viewings, some people told me, 'You've got to be strong for your parents' sake,' " David Hayhurst recalls. "Hogwash." That is not David's way of saying he didn't respect his folks' grief; it is merely his way of expressing that he, too, had pains to contend with. No one was as intimately linked with all five of the youngsters who died as David had been. David lost both of his brothers, at a time when they had become close friends instead of rivals. He had lived next door to Tommy, whose Christian walk he respected greatly. David had worked with Eric that summer and had spent many an hour talking with his new friend. And he had shared spiritual matters and correspondence with Maria, as part of what had become very much of a big brother–little sister relationship. It was almost impossible for David to turn in any direction without having memories come whizzing at him like so many sharp-edged Frisbees.

"As a senior in high school, I pretty much ran the activity end of the youth group at our church," David says. "But that was about all we had at the time. I had also been involved in our family taping ministry, in another youth group, and in several Bible studies. But Christ wasn't really sinking in. I had always been the 'good little kid.' Now it [accepting Christ and the Christian lifestyle] is a decision *I* have made. When I was a freshman in college, the Campus Crusade for Christ Bible studies that I went to helped to make Christ part of my reality and my daily life. At this time I finally started to have devotions every day. The night of the accident, I was hanging around in the hall of my dorm, joking around, laughing, throwing a Frisbee. I got back to my room about 2:00 or 2:30 in the morning. My roommate was asleep. I wondered if I should have my devotions. It was so late, but I had them anyway. I read 1 Peter 5 that night. After I got the call in the morning about the accident, I looked up those verses again. They applied so perfectly to my situation. It was such a comfort, especially verse 10 about Christ Himself strengthening and lifting me up from my suffering.

"I had a hard time dealing with the accident, but I didn't show it as much as some others did. My eyes would often be filled with tears, but I rarely wept outright. I dealt with it inwardly a lot. A great deal of my strength came from my friends. We kind of leaned on each other, since each of us—myself, Rob [Grieve], Beth [Robertson], and Laurie [Cole]—had our own elements of suffering to deal with. My fellowship with these three, as well as with my roommate and other Christian friends at school, was the source of both comfort and strength. I can't say enough about the importance of Christian fellowship in handling grief. The chance to have someone to talk to, to just open up and let it all out, means so much.

"The accident both helped and hurt my walk with the Lord. It helped me to get to the point where I could talk with Him as I talk with another person. In my time of stress, I didn't have the patience or desire to get formal. It's helped me to be able to open up to Him like I would to a close friend. But my walk with the Lord isn't back to where it should be. My daily devotions fizzled out soon after the accident. Even today I struggle with consistency. But at least I haven't lost sight of Him. The accident helped to make me aware that there was more to life and fulfillment than a high-paying job. I realized that people are important and that the Lord's will for my life should come before my future salary. That was part of the reason for me leaving the engineering program at Rutgers for human communications, and for my plans to go to Bible school. It's become important for me to know Him personally, to know His Word, and to know His will for my life."

Howard and Mary Jane Borloz did not think Andy would care to express himself about what he had gone through. To their surprise, Andy did. Andy, who is now working as an exhibit product designer for a design firm in northern New Jersey, took pen in hand and printed a summary of his feelings. This is what he wrote:

"The first few months after the accident were very difficult. I was struggling with the pain of separation. I went to work on Monday after Eric's death and the people in the office thought I was crazy to come to work. All I wanted to do was to keep myself busy so I wouldn't feel the pain of Eric's loss. My boss wouldn't leave me alone while I was working and he was dumping his unneeded sympathies on me. I had told him that he need not say he was sorry all the time. Not paying any attention to what I was saying, his reply was: 'But, oh Andy, I'm soooo sorry. I know how you feel. I felt the same way when my dog died.' I couldn't wait to get home and laugh about that.

"Two months later, I lost the job. I had kept myself so busy I almost forgot about my emotional pain. After I was let go, I went home and the pain became much harder to bear. Many nights I wept alone in my bedroom, not wanting my parents to see me upset over the double loss.

"For a long time, I attempted to fill my void by buying a lot of books and magazines about design, theology, management, and cooking, and also biographies. I couldn't stand the pain of having a hole in my life, so I tried to 'narcotize' the pain by escaping into my reading. I'm now learning how to let God fill my void with His love instead of filling it by myself with books. Books could never completely satisfy the needs I have the way God can.

"One night, I confessed to God my thoughts about Eric. I thought Eric was mine to keep for the rest of my life. It meant a lot to me to have a younger brother. In order for my wounds to be healed, I had to let him go to God and let God have him.

"The most frustrating part of my grieving process is the lack of available listeners. . . . I thank God that I have found several—especially Betty and Gene Addison. They pray for me daily and care about my feelings, my job, and my life.

"Three years after the death of Eric, my church congregation was asked during the service to pray for the parents of the four families. The brothers and sisters of the deceased were not mentioned. I was at that service and I felt left out."

"I cried a lot after the accident," says Bonnie Furman, who used to be one of the mainstays of the youth group. "All of us cried. A lot of kids thought about death and their own dying after that. We all knew it could have happened to *any* of us because any of us could have been in that van.

"Nobody gets experienced about death. It's a shock. It's sadness. Then you move on. The biggest thing for me was looking at life and seeing how temporary it is. It blew me away. There was a feeling of futility. But there is hope as a Christian that I'll see those kids again in heaven.

"The first two weeks after the accident, everyone was very consoling to the kids in the youth group. Then all the kids were crushed because the older people didn't help us any longer. We tried to remain a group, but our foundation had been taken out from underneath us. We'd come through a difficult time and nobody sensed our group needed help, support. It was not right for them to think we should just march on as if nothing had happened. We felt so sorry for the parents. Rob Grieve started calling Mrs. Hayhurst 'Mom.' We knew there was such a tremendous void in their lives. We wanted to move in with them and show them our love. But we knew nothing would ever replace their two sons. It's hard to look at the parents. You know they look at you and think of their own kids. I can see the sadness in Mr. Van Beers' eyes, the other parents' eyes. I think Mr. Van Beers carries the sadness on his face, too. I go to the church and I feel so sad. There has to be a point where you don't feel so sad all the time. So when I'm home from college now, I don't even go to the church."

During the summer following the accident, Tim Biscaye worked on the same Teen Missions field in Honduras where Mark Hayhurst had labored the year before. "One reason I went was because of Mark," Tim explains. "He had grown up so much during the summer he was there. I could see it. It was also an adventuresome thing to do.

"One of my first responses after the accident was, 'There's glory in death.' I was angry the Lord didn't think I was good enough to be taken. Verbalizing my emotions has been hard. I saw myself as the kind who would let the girls cry on his shoulder. But Tim wouldn't cry. Tim *didn't* cry. I wanted people to lean on me. But I didn't have the maturity I needed and I didn't know that you have to let out your emotions."

"At first, I felt guilty," Laurie Cole says. "If the meeting had been at my house the way it had been scheduled, there wouldn't have been an accident. For a while, I had nightmares. There was one I kept having over and over. The nightmare starts with all of us kids in the van. Brian and I have a mock fight and he says, 'OK, get out.' I get out. The van goes a few feet. There's an accident. All five of the kids are dead.

"Now I go to another youth group at another church. One reason I stopped going [to the Pascack Bible Church] was because *everything* related back to the accident. It was all we talked about. It was important to talk about it, but it didn't seem to help us. But the accident did hurry me along as a Christian. I had accepted Christ on our retreat to Boston not long before the accident. Because of the accident, I *really* came to know the Lord. The strength I saw in the Hayhursts and the Van Beerses after the accident showed me a lot about their love for the Lord."

"Not a day goes by that I don't think about Maria," says Beth Robertson, who was her best friend. "Mrs. Van Beers gave me a five-by-seven picture of Maria that I have in my room at college. I still hold the same religious beliefs I did before, but I find that the church is not the same any more. Too big."

"What got me was that as I came out of the side door of the church after the funeral services, there were the television people trying to get some of the youngsters on camera," Bob McCarthy says. "Before you knew it, it was like moths rushing to a light. They formed a circle and put their arms around each other. They said, 'Yes, we are one together.' There were a lot of kids saying things like, 'Hallelujah!' and 'Praise the Lord' and all that victory talk. They had just come out of an emotional service and I'm sure they all did feel they were one together. Soon, though, there was a division of ranks. It was like a show. Notoriety had been creeping in even before the funeral. There was a lot of interest in who got his or her name in the newspaper, who was quoted. I don't mean to portray the kids as being insincere. They really meant it when they said things like, 'We love the Lord,' and 'Through God all things are possible,' and 'Our friends are in heaven with Jesus right now and we *know* it.' Some of them had been taught that in Sunday School and had heard it for years. But now they had to back up their words with their lives, with the way they would live. A lot of the young people later said, 'I opened my mouth and said things I couldn't live up to.'"

Jan McCarthy added these observations: "The first night the youth group met after the accident, some of the kids asked, 'What if I'm next?' [The McCarthys, as they had promised Maria at the previous meeting, played a tape by Betty Malz, the woman who had been "dead" for twenty-eight minutes. A few of the youngsters said they were impressed by it; the rest said it did nothing to help them spiritually or emotionally. This rather negative reaction may have been because, as Jan put it, "The kids were emotionally low."] Frankly, there was a very dissenting spirit among them. It got so bad that about six months after the accident I gave them a lecture about their tongues. One night, they had a minor food fight at Friendly's. Suddenly, they weren't the same lovely, wonderful group of kids who had been going to Friendly's all the time. There was also a phone call from a Park Ridge police captain. 'What's happening with your youth group?' he wanted to know. It wasn't that the kids were in trouble with the police, but this man had heard negative things about the group and he was surprised because he had known the group and that the kids had always been so lovely. We'd plan activities for the group and many of the kids wouldn't show up because they weren't speaking to one another."

"I've had nightmares about the accident," Patrolman Gary Ahlers said early in 1982. "Not long after the accident, I was hospitalized because of nervous tension and internal disorders. The doctor said the accident could have subconsciously touched it all off. I was in the hospital ten days. Two months later, my troubles were back and I was in the hospital for seven days. My wife says that she's heard me cry in my sleep."

On Sunday morning, November 12, 1978, a husband and wife were at the Archer United Methodist Church in Allendale. Reverend Clark David Callender of that church approached them and asked them to return to their home with him. When they arrived there, a police officer told the couple that their only two sons had been killed in an accident the night before. That was the way Harlan and Phyllis Stricklett got the news. At the memorial service for the men, Reverend Callender referred to Stuart Stricklett as "perhaps the true pacifist" and mentioned his "deep family ties." Of Roger Stricklett the minister said he was a person "who wrestled with life . . . the artist-builder." Harlan Stricklett was quoted in a local newspaper as saying, "As a Christian, I have to believe that death is a victorious thing. I believe it strongly enough that it guides my life and, I hope, my dying."

Essentially, this book is about the five youngsters from the Pascack Bible Church, their families, friends, and the church itself. What, though, of the Stricketts? Harlan Stricklett was extremely reluctant to be interviewed when he was contacted in January of 1982. Then he relented. It would have to be a short session, he indicated. And his wife did not wish to be interviewed at all. Harlan Stricklett was sixty-two at the time of the crash. Phyllis was fifty-seven. Discussing the tragedy, he said over the phone, was still very painful for both of them. When he opened a door at the back of the house a few minutes later, Harlan motioned to a chair at the nearby kitchen table. He sat on the other side of the table, his face marvelously ruddy, his hair superbly white. When he spoke, it was with carefully chosen words and, at times, with a voice that quavered with emotion.

"Our greatest strength has been that we are Christians," Harlan Stricklett began. "It [the accident] gave our church a chance to become a community of love. I got up one day and thanked the congregation for letting Jesus walk among us during the first week after the accident when so many reached out to us. At the memorial service for the boys, the parents of the other children came and extended their sympathy and Christian love. It was *very* moving for us.

"It's been painful to live with and still is. But I'm able to talk about it now, which is something I was not able to do for a long time." Harlan had his elbows on the table, had knitted his fingers together and placed his chin on the bridge formed by his interlocked hands. This was to become a ritual he would indulge in when he could feel that he was on the verge of tears. In his voice at these times there seemed to be a mist.

"I suppose our Christian life has been deeper and more meaningful since this experience. There's been more of a close feeling with Christ as a result. And certainly our feeling toward our congregation and church is different. Now we feel a kinship. It must be hard if one is not a Christian. How you could cope with it [death], I don't know.

"It is difficult to explain the terrific shock and pain that one undergoes. If one couldn't believe in life hereafter and in the forgiveness of Christ, the whole experience would be shattering. They [members of the church, friends, neighbors] did about everything you could think of when it was needed most. They brought us flowers, plants, wreaths, food. One young man, who was a friend of one of the boys in high school, became like an adopted son to us at that time. We hadn't known him that well before, but he kept coming by to see us. Now he's getting his doctorate as a clinical psychologist. We saw him when he was home at Thanksgiving. He wrapped his arms around me just like I was his father.

"We also received communications from people in the Chicago church we went to twenty years ago. They'd heard about it. There were various expressions from all sorts of people. That helps take your mind off the problems. It's after that is over that the grief takes control. When you're alone or only with another family member, it sometimes is hard. My wife and I helped each other. We did a lot of Scripture reading together and we prayed together."

Harlan Stricklett talked about his recent retirement after a career in the public health field. He mentioned that he grew up on a farm near Mitchell, South Dakota, and that when he was eighteen the Depression and the Dust Bowl forced him and his family to move to Sioux Falls. Speaking of the accident again, he said: "There are times when it still becomes very poignant. Certain dates—birthdays, anniversaries, Christmas, Thanksgiving. We see things around the house that remind us of the departed ones.

"I was baptized in '41. I've had ups and downs as a Christian since then," he says with a waggle of his hand to emphasize that there have been extreme highs and extreme lows. "There have been many tears. I'm an emotional sort, so it doesn't take much for me. The pain was the most severe during the first year. It moderated somewhat during the second year and has become acceptable in the third year. A sense of realization grows in one that you can't change anything. You accept your hopes on the basis of faith. As a Christian, you feel sure of the resurrection and that you'll someday be rejoicing with your loved ones. This comes as you get older and come closer to the point of death yourself.

"Advertisers lead us in the direction of making Americans believe they'll never die, that we'll always be young and that we'll live forever. Even churches don't do much in the way of preparing people for the inevitability of death. I like to feel I'm prepared for death, as long as I can believe God has forgiven me and will accept me as I am. Some verses in the Bible have helped. Don't know that I can quote them. One is, 'I go to prepare a place for you . . . if it were not so, I would have told you.' Another is, 'For God so loved the world. . . .'

"The boys were involved with the church earlier as children. 'Born again' is a term that sort of irks me. I believe that if you're a Christian you must be born again. Christ said it. How can you profess to be a Christian if you're not born again? Therefore, all Christians have to be born again. When I was first baptized, I felt I'd accepted Jesus Christ at the moving of the Holy Spirit, not of my own volition. I was surprised to find myself going forward. This was in a Baptist Church in Sioux Falls, South Dakota."

A buzzer on the kitchen stove sounded off. Dinner was ready. The conversation was over.

17

An Old Milk Carton
and a New Vision

Fred Beveridge had entered the ministry with the enthusiasm of a rookie baseball player breaking into the major leagues. Before the end of his first four years as pastor of a church in Massachusetts, however, he felt he had been a big strikeout. Three distinct "strikes" almost turned him into a ministerial dropout.

Strike One—Having to deal with the depth of pain that some people must go through brought a realization of his own lack of equipment in certain areas of ministry. The death of one of his parishioners shook Beveridge from the top of his head full of black hair to the soles of his size ten feet.

Strike Two—The charismatic controversy was cropping up all over the place. In his own church there were only slight repercussions, but college students off at Christian schools wrote asking for advice on it. Beveridge's counsel was always the same. "It's bad news and unbiblical—stay away," was his constant reply. "My seminary education was intensely preoccupied with the study of Scripture," he now says. "With regard to the miraculous gifts of the Holy Spirit, however, theology overruled and the point was emotionally argued that these gifts had passed from the scene with the apostles. In preaching this as doctrine in my evangelical church, I ended up driving out a family that came out of an Assembly of God background. I had caused for them a problem that up to that time did not exist. My lack of love and understanding of the complexities of the issue had caused a breach in fellowship. I resolved to study the issue more deeply."

Strike Three—Fred had a prevailing feeling that he had been a flop as a minister. He sums it up this way: "I failed to help unify a growing church. As the congregation grew, it grew into two factions. One loyal to Fred Beveridge, and one loyal to a relatively unhealthy traditionalism. Instead of working to heal the rift, I revelled in the affection of my group and allowed them to 'defend' me, thus further polarizing the factions. My desire to succeed caused me to fail. I was not happy about the way my pastorate concluded there, and I was emotionally and spiritually broken by the experience."

At that time, the Pascack Bible Church in New Jersey had been in touch with him about becoming its pastor. His desire was to stay and start a new church from among his supporters in Massachusetts, but the thought of schism sickened him. He found the church in New Jersey to be an exciting "out," except for one thing: It had had a full-scale controversy over the charismatic issue in 1971, and the rift was still far from healed. Beveridge knew the pain that the former pastor had gone through with the congregation and he was wary of his own ability, especially at this time in his life, to handle the stress. "I remember the sick feeling I had in the pit of my stomach when I realized I had accepted the pastorate of a church with such a ready-made tinder box. I was so personally hurt in Massachusetts, that I didn't believe I could be any good for anybody."

Christians often speak about peak-and-valley periods of spiritual fluctuation—high-as-a-mountain experiences and low-as-the-lowest-valley trials are common. Obviously, what Dr. Beveridge needed at the outset of his ministry in New Jersey was a mountaintop experience. Where, though, would he get one? On top of a mountain, that's where. A mountain? Mountains are never there when you need them. In August 1975, the Beveridges moved to New Jersey and a week after moving in, Fred had an unplanned mountaintop episode—with a real mountain, too. Before assuming the pulpit for the first time at PBC, he had to fulfill a prior commitment at a Bible conference, where he was to be a speaker and musician. A guest cottage was provided with its own cooking facilities. He had not been aware that these were the arrangements. Dr. Beveridge says, "I decided that this would be an excellent opportunity to spend my free time praying for my new pastorate, and working through some of my own feelings about the pastorate. There, on the shores of Alton Bay jutting off of Lake Winnipesaukee, I walked and talked with the Lord about my own spiritual life and my attitude toward the pastorate. Nearby was a challenging three-mile trail up the rocky side of Mt. Major. That mountain became my mountain. I sang, recited Scripture, and praised God as I never had before on that hike up the side of Major. One afternoon as I broke through the tree line and saw the whole panorama of the glistening lake before me, God began to lift the fog from my heart. He took

Scriptures that I had known and He retaught them to me. It was an extraordinary experience in New Hampshire.

"I took an old milk carton I found on the way, and scratched a few notes on it with an old golf pencil that was in my pocket. That night I scribbled page after page of impressions that the Holy Spirit had left in my heart up on Mt. Major. They were impressions all directly related to the Body of Christ, what it should be, what my attitude should be as a pastor. The Scriptures were arranged for me by the Holy Spirit in such a way that I knew God had a particular place for me in the church and that he was going to use me as a catalyst for its renewal in a very specific way."

What Beveridge jotted down on an old milk carton and later on paper gave him ammunition for a battle he had thought he was entering virtually unarmed. "In 1971 there had been a division in the congregation caused by some immature attitudes on both sides of the charismatic issue," Beveridge says. "This is inevitable as new issues arise. Working through them takes time, patience, love, and divine wisdom. The charismatics were pushy because of their new power and love for the Lord. Theirs they saw as the only way. A backlash developed and there were, as the story goes, hostilities that almost irretrievably affected the church."

Beveridge launched into his new ministry with a new vision. It began with a series of sermons on the nature of the Church as described in 1 Peter and an evening series on discipleship, unity (John 17), and Christian fellowship. By October the vision was outlined in practical fashion for the Governing Body and it was enthusiastically endorsed. The effort was to include a restructuring of the church leadership to involve laymen as part of the pastoral team. The heavy load of "church work" was to be shifted to doing the "work of the church," and the congregation was to be broken down into pastoral units called undershepherd groups. The move was one of decentralization. That direction was accepted enthusiastically by most of the congregation.

"Unexpectedly, it brought many charismatics and noncharismatics together and established a dialogue and a mutual appreciation," says Beveridge. "There was growth in the direction of a healthy unity, but there always remained an undercurrent of suspicion that would break forth as a result of a raised hand, an amen, or a Scripture chorus sung spontaneously in one of our services. All these expressions were orderly, but beyond our tradition. Feelings often ran high as the emotions of the past flooded into the present.

"The congregation grew, slowly at first, and then more rapidly. Many of the people won to Christ were friends and relatives of those in thriving undershepherd groups. Several of the groups got so large that we had to divide and add new undershepherds. We could not, however, stay ahead of the pace of growth. Finally we just added small groups with group leaders. We called them Care-Rings. Many of the people coming into PBC during this period were former Roman Catholics who had been won to faith by outreach ministries of PBC and through the Roman Catholic charismatic renewal. They brought with them their relational bent, their rejection of formality, their enthusiasm for the Lord, and a new type of exuberance that was expressed outwardly. These were not 'tongues-speaking' charismatics out of traditional protestantism or evangelicalism. These were people who loved everybody who loved Jesus. Their zeal was a threat to some, an inspiration to others. I found myself pastoring two congregations again."

It took courage for Beveridge to maintain his vision for a church with visible unity through this period. A breakthrough came in the middle of it while on a Governing Body/undershepherd retreat at Tuscarora in the Pocono Mountains of Pennsylvania.

This church which had known division and its pain on two recent occasions was discovering that schism seems to breed schism. It had to be stopped somewhere. In October 1977, forgiveness swept through the leadership body gathered together in that retreat center in the Poconos. Factions that were once embittered toward one another were healed, forgiveness flowed, and they returned a united group of leaders.

During 1978 it was left for the leadership to try to interpret what had happened to the body. By autumn the need for further clarification was apparent, so the Governing Body and undershepherds departed on the third annual retreat, this time to Ocean Grove, New Jersey, where the summary conclusions were hammered out. PBC would be a unified congregation, including balanced and biblical charismatics, and tolerant, growing evangelicals. Whatever the Holy Spirit was to bring, as judged by the leadership, was to be accepted. Pastor Beveridge said, "It was not easy to express this conclusion to the congregation. As a matter of fact, I think our stumbling attempt to articulate it to the congregation during a Sunday evening service was more harmful than helpful. It set loose some fear that had been bottled up in the congregation for some time. The issue of just what kind of congregation we were to be was once again a matter of debate among the people. No one was really satisfied. In addition, other things were happening. Our youth minister's wife, who was a young Christian herself, and too immature to take the pressures of being so close to the ministry, bolted for her home in Boston. There was no opportunity at that time for reconciliation. We truly felt we were under full attack. The missiles started hitting and we had little to do but huddle together in prayer. Then came the accident. I wondered that night whether PBC would survive it. Two charismatic families, two noncharismatic families. How would they take it, what would they say to each other, what kind of statement would be made to the whole church, what would the members of the congregation express to those families based upon our evident divisions? My fears were unfounded. Tragedy pointed out one overriding truth—when push comes to shove, family is family. You are one when you are under fire—you have no choice."

18

How to Help

"God has given us memories that we may have roses in December"

The above words conjure up a lovely mental picture, which is surely what James M. Barrie had in mind when he wrote them specifically for those who grieve. Those people, though, know that roses have, amid their loveliness, thorns. How to enjoy the roses without being hurt by the thorns is just one of the many complexities of the grieving process.

Our limited knowledge about how to cope with death stems largely from the fact that we know so little about how to *think* about it and how to *talk* about it. We contemplate and discuss numerous topics—the high cost of living, the weather, politics, jobs, health, crabgrass. But when it comes to death, it seems we would rather die than think or talk about it. It is time we learned how to do both.

Pastor Beveridge and the four families have, collectively, spent thousands of hours trying to learn more about grief and death. And yet none has the magic answer that will simplify grief and bring it to a swift end. That's because there is no simple solution. Dealing with grief is, at best, an inexact process, partly because everyone suffers through its stages differently. There is, though, much that these people have found out. Although the grief spawned by death is the subject of these pages, this information should be useful to those who grieve for other reasons—divorce, a job loss, separation, illness, a move, a broken romance.

From the beginning, one of the main objectives of this book has been to give the four families and Pastor Beveridge a chance to express what they have learned. It has also been the intent to have the comments of these people stand mostly by themselves rather than compare them with clinical and professional observations by others. It has been the prayer of all concerned that they will have portrayed themselves in ways that will enable you to know how much they want to help you deal with your present or future grief. One request: think and/or talk about what this chapter says to you. Learning often requires repetition, so re-read the bits of advice that follow. And, when the time comes when *you* are grieving, prayerfully read the advice of these people, who with all their hearts and all their love are reaching out to you.

Several years ago in the Northeast, a minister turned to the surviving family members during a funeral service and said, "I don't know what to say that will be of any real comfort to you." It seemed like an appalling statement. It may, however, have been the most honest statement he could have made. We tend to think that clergymen can deal with death in majestic ways and that they can summon up words that will—Presto!—provide lasting comfort that will banish grief forever. Can any of them really do that? It is doubtful. If there *is* someone who can accomplish that, the world needs that person to step forward right now to minister to its suffering millions.

"I had absolutely no training about how to help the grieving," says Dr. Beveridge of all his years of schooling for the ministry. No preparation for handling the most painful situation that many parishioners will ever have to face! Is a minister supposed to tell mourners, "I don't know what to say that will be of any real comfort to you"? That might fly once, but after that, it's all crash landings.

There is, thankfully, hope. It stems from a new consciousness of death and grief that may be an offshoot from growing fears people have about their own safety, about the possibility of nuclear war, and about the approach of Armageddon. Observing death and hearing about it has become an everyday event for many people because radio, television, Hollywood, and the press inundate us with stories that dote on death. It has taken far too long, but at last there has come this awareness that death—as a topic we must all face, not as a media event—is something almost no one is prepared to deal with. Pastor Beveridge became aware that many people, including himself, were at a loss when it came to ministering to the four families. As a result, he was the moderator for two Sunday evening services in May 1980, forums that dealt with death, grief, and how to help those who sorrow.

"I don't see much difference between the pain of mourning for the Christian and the non-Christian," was Pastor Beveridge's surprising observation after one forum. It is a valid one, though, and one he backed up by adding, "The obvious promise is that the Christians' loss is not ultimate ["ye sorrow not, even as others who have no hope," 1 Thessalonians 4:13] because if their loved ones have given their lives to Christ there is the promise that they'll be reunited in heaven. That's the ultimate consolation. But the *pain* of the believer who grieves is just as real as it is for the nonbeliever. Larry Carroll is the only exception I know of. He walks with complete and utter victory. This doesn't mean he doesn't care, but he is not ruled by his emotions. Nothing can get that man down. That's because he lives so close to the breast of the Lord. Some of the others still have much pain. I wish I could lift their grief. Connie expressed to me once that perhaps I had not been all to her and Walt that I could have been. She had read a book about what a pastor should do, and I didn't measure up to all of it. I felt very bad. As I sat across from her, I wept and she wept, and we both recognized we were communicating and that there really wasn't any distance between us after all. I confess to not knowing how to help those four families any more than I have. I ministered in every way I knew. I bled with them. But I'm sure I failed in some areas."

According to the parents, Pastor Beveridge was more successful at ministering to them than he realized. Some of the parents felt there were limits to how much he could do, for he had a whole congregation and a family of his own to tend to. And, in a very real way, he grieved with the families.

Then, too, there was the suddenness of the loss. There were no last goodbyes, not even final glimpses. Suddenly, loved ones were memories, pictures on mantels or in wallets. Barbara Hayhurst said, "I'm not sure that all of me has fully accepted the fact that they won't somehow come back." Don Hayhurst added this thought: "Part of the difficulty was that the kids were so young and that their deaths were so sudden."

"Christians sometimes have a light touch on life," Pastor Beveridge said. "I hear people encourage each other to think there is no pain or suffering for the believer, that Christians shouldn't weep or grieve. There is nothing un-Christian about recognizing the tragic elements of life. After all, life is not a melodrama in which God is always riding on a white horse to deliver us from difficulties. That certainly wasn't the case in the life of Jesus. But believers have the comfort of the promise that if they are absent from this body they will be present with the Lord. We still don't know all we'd like to know about how this takes place, but we are assured that after our death there is a conscious existence that continues with Christ. That's something we can rejoice about. But we also have to realize that there is a time to weep. We are told that Jesus wept. He identified with human suffering and with the pain of death, and He wasn't afraid to weep. One of the most comforting thoughts has been the realization that God loved those five youngsters as much as their families or anyone else did."

Many people have commented about how they wished they had been able to help the families more with their grief. How to do this has befuddled even some of the most sincere of them. People are so uncertain about what to do or what not to do. Three years after the accident, Nedaleine Biscaye said, "When I see those families, my first sensation is one of pain." Despite that, she had the courage to try to help. The time she has spent with the parents, her concern, her kindnesses large and small—they have all been definite helps. She was not the only one who was of aid. Pat Stark was surprised to learn that she had been of *any* assistance to Barbara Hayhurst, who early in '82 said, "Pat's *still* helping me. She's willing to listen. Some people say they want to help, but you can tell they really don't. Others say, 'I've had a burden to pray for you. Is everything all right?' They're the special ones. Some people want to reach out, but you can sense they're afraid of getting involved. Pat's not afraid to listen. And she's willing to be open about her own needs."

For Connie Van Beers, the most consistent source of comfort was farther away—in New Canaan, Connecticut. That's where the Hillmeyers live. "Sherry Hillmeyer and Maria were close friends until Sherry's family moved to Connecticut," Connie says. "After the accident Sherry became almost a replacement for Maria. She visited here, called, wrote, made herself available to listen. Betty—her mother—invited me to 'come cry on my shoulder.' Several times I did. I drove an hour-and-a-quarter to New Canaan to talk with her and open up."

"The congregation was uneasy about how to minister to these families," Pastor Beveridge says. "People didn't know what to do, what to say. I didn't know what to do. For two years, every time I got in the pulpit and prayed, I felt I *had* to pray for the families, make some remark about the five kids. In almost every service, I reminded the congregation to uphold the families in prayer. And yet I'm not sure how well we as a congregation ministered in terms of long-term care. I believe that what we have to learn from the accident is not yet finished."

The two surest ways to be of aid are these: be there and be available. Those who grieve seem to seldom seek help from others, not wishing to burden others. Make no mistake about it; there *is* a burden that grievers carry and those who want to help must be willing to bear part of that load. The rewards, however, are worth it.

If you are beginning to see that dealing with grief is a two-way road, then you are well on the way to appreciating what it is all about. It is, though, a unique highway with road signs that have unconventional meanings. SOFT SHOULDER has nothing to do with the condition of the edge of the highway. Instead, it refers to the shoulder that must be kept ready for the grieving person to weep on. CURVE AHEAD and STEEP HILL are warnings that, even though both parties are trying their best, there may be difficulties. *Wanting* to help and *being able* to help are different things. It may take time for both sides to figure out how to handle the situation in which they are now joined. What's more, listening is not easy. It is possible to listen without hearing and this insincerity will do more harm than good. Some people, despite their efforts, are not good hearers. If you're one of them, you can still be of aid. How? By letting the griever know that you want to help (that surely would be nice to know), that you'd be glad to go shopping, have lunch, or do any of a dozen other things (having a friend who will do this is a blessing).

The most important sign along this highway is the one that says BE HONEST. If you find that handling another's burden becomes too heavy for you, then it's time to be honest enough to say, "That's about all I can handle right now. I want to help you, but if I get dragged down I won't be able to." Keep in mind that those who grieve definitely want to talk about other things, just as you want to hear about other things. They want to be assured that they are still part of the world that has been so severely jarred for them. And remember that they are willing to listen, too; willing to know that you have problems, too. It's a long highway and if you are going to travel it together, then honesty is a must.

Can you really be of help? Walt Van Beers answers that by saying, "The help comes from knowing that people care. It *really* helps." So call someone who's grieving and ask if they'd like you to come over or if they'd like to come to your place or if they'd like to go out for lunch or a walk. Pop in for a surprise visit. Write a letter. The Van Beerses took special delight from cards that several people sent them on the third anniversary of the accident. Why? Because it is important for grieving people to know their loved ones have not been forgotten by others. Pastor Beveridge and the families felt that some of the finest displays of Christian love were the spontaneous, spur-of-the-moment ones. Should you give someone a hug when you know that person is hurting? Absolutely. Should you bake a cake or bring flowers to those who mourn? Absolutely. If you don't, who will? And even if others do those things, what can be wrong with showing that you care and want to reach out? Many people have mentioned that they feel "uneasy" about trying to assist those who sorrow. Well, it's natural to feel that way about a delicate matter like this, especially when you don't know what you are getting into.

"People who grieve need to talk about their loved ones who have died, need to keep their memories alive," Pastor Beveridge points out. "I had thought it was best to forget and move on. But it is vital to keep alive the fact that the person who died was an important part of one's life.

"After Steven had died when he was three months old, people would stop any conversation about babies if I was in the room," Barbara Hayhurst says. "That *crushed* me. We have learned this time around, especially since people don't know where you're at and whether you want them to talk about your loved one or not, that it's *up to us* to start such conversations. If *you* mention the child or spouse or parent you lost, then people feel free to talk about that person. Otherwise, people have no way of knowing. We change, though. One day we're one way, the next day we might be the opposite."

"I felt the Lord was punishing me," Connie Van Beers says. "I couldn't think of any other reason why He would have taken Maria. I remember vividly that I prayed, because I felt I was a very weak Christian, that the Lord would put me through a test. I prayed this prayer *every* night for quite a while before the accident. I can honestly tell you that through all this I have become a much stronger Christian."

"I hated God for a time," Walt Van Beers adds. "I told Him He was a zero, that He couldn't hack it, that He was a loser. Finally, God brought me to the place where I could see that my anger wasn't going to change anything. That's when I decided He could handle things. All of us are leaving some day. There are only two possibilities: Either Jesus is the last great fairy tale or He's exactly what He says He is. I thank God every day for those who helped so much during the early days after the accident. The honesty of some people's comments has helped, too. A few days before the first Christmas after the accident, Joan Van Der Werf said to me, 'I *wish* you a merry Christmas but I know in my heart you're not going to have one.' That's an honest, from-the-heart remark. A remark to stay away from is, 'It should have happened to us. I think we might have been able to handle it better than you.' Baloney. You *never* want it to happen to you."

"There were some well-meaning people who said to our two remaining children, 'Be strong for your parents,' " Barbara Hayhurst says. "Well, those youngsters needed to be able to sorrow, too.

"You have to be willing to share, to share that you *are* hurting. When you hurt so much that you raise up a wall and don't share, then you go down and others can't be used by the Lord to bring you the help you need. The body of believers was far more important in our healing than any of us realized."

"The accident made it possible for people in the church to express love they otherwise couldn't or wouldn't have shared," Mary Jane Borloz says. "It has brought friendship to us. It has brought love to us from people we never expected it from. I could see that there were people who felt a loss, just as we did. And I could see them reaching out. There was always someone with the right word or a hug or a kiss. I think it surprised some of them that they could give that much and that they could *really* feel they were helping us."

In *For Those Who Hurt,* Chuck Swindoll writes, "We cannot prepare for a crisis *after* that crisis occurs. Preparation must take place *before* we are nose to nose with the issue." A highly logical statement. It is the sort of logic that is rarely applied to preparing ourselves for dealing with grief, which is what Swindoll had in mind. *Now* is the time for us to begin the getting-ready process.

"Sometimes I just have to let myself be overwhelmed," David Hayhurst says.

Don Hayhurst has found it extremely helpful to deal with one memory at a time because, "Each time it comes back it's less painful than before." After a disappointment some three years after the accident, Don went into another form of grief. "Tim LaHaye's book, *How To Win Over Depression,* helped me see that I was being devastated by bitterness and self pity," he says. "I finally took the situation to the Lord and since then I've been able to make progress." Don took time to write down the following:

A few important spiritual lessons learned since November 11, 1978: During a dry spell or a time of distress, continue steadfastly in that to which you committed yourself to when you were spiritually attuned. Continue to fellowship with the body of believers where you have found meaningful relationships. They will encourage you and pray for you. You will draw strength from them. Be careful not to carry over-burdening responsibilities that result in an overtaxing of spiritual strength. To try to give out spiritual strength, when there is none or very little left to give, can be disastrous to one's inner spirit. This is not the time to make a show of strength that isn't there, but a time to openly confess your need for support and ministry. This honesty with yourself and others may require putting off some of the responsibilities you have been carrying. We may not understand what we are going through, so the only thing left for us is to say, as Job of old said, 'Though he slay me, yet will I trust him.' God needs a people who will walk in His love and will let Him live through them. There is power in obedience.

Why do Christians, even the strongest ones, grieve? It is because our humanity dominates all of us; we are, above all else, mere mortals. Death shocks us like nothing else. After the initial jolt comes death's stealthy ally, grief. As deep-cutting as grief is, it is a vital part of the healing mechanism. The danger of grief is that one can become trapped in its catacombs: depression, prolonged anger, guilt, extensive mourning, and a sense of "lostness." People are frequently unaware of how deep they fall into some of those pits. The "lostness" is a reference to out-of-touch-with-reality behavior. Some senses are heightened by grief; others are dulled. Those who go through lostness are shocked to learn about some of the things they did while caught up in it. Rising above grief is one thing; staying there is another. "We must keep our eyes on the Lord," Larry Carroll says as he explains how he has, for the most part, been able to rise above. Speaking of himself, he adds a truth that can be applied to all: "If I take my eyes off the Lord, I'll stumble."

The death of a child is often the most painful to endure. In Harriet Sarnoff Schiff's book, *The Bereaved Parent,* she quotes these incisive words from Dr. Elliott Luby: "When your parent dies, you have lost your past. When your child dies, you have lost your future." Much the same is true for those who lose a spouse, for part of the past is lost and dreams of the future are shattered.

Negotiating the valley of grief is like trying to weave through a minefield, which can be accomplished successfully only if one has supreme good fortune or a map of where the mines are. Members of all four families have testified that they would not have made it as far as they have had it not been for the help of those who ministered to them and had it not been for the strength they found in their Christian faith.

Imagining others' grief is not easy. To better comprehend their pain, it might be worth thinking about how you would feel if *you* had lost a loved one. Unfortunately, we often take little time to think. We are so busy with life that we don't have time to prepare for death. Discussing grief with those who have gone through it or who are in the midst of it is an excellent way to learn about it. Most such people will talk about it. They'll gladly open up. Doing so may also be therapeutic for grievers because it can help them understand themselves and their plight. Another fine way to learn is to minister to those who sorrow.

What should you do or not do? If there is any "no no," it is thinking that you can help by sermonizing. A Bible verse or two is sufficient. There are many appropriate ones, such as Isaiah 25:8: "He will swallow up death in victory; and the Lord God will wipe away tears from all faces." Or Revelation 14:13: "Blessed are the dead who die in the Lord. . . ."

The easiest thing to find is an excuse and if you find one for not trying to help those who grieve, then it's likely you'll find more. All of us would be appalled if we knew how much we have hurt grievers by *not* even trying to help. If you are not sure what to do, ask them how you can be of assistance. Work at *hearing* what they say. It's easier to give words than to receive them, but being a good listener will often be the most important thing you can do.

19

Why?

"When I first heard about the accident on Sunday morning, I broke down and I asked the Lord, 'Why?' At church that morning, several young people ran up to me in the parking lot and asked, 'Why?' " So says Bob Paton, an elder at the Pascack Bible Church. "Why?" is the most natural question to ask after tragedies such as the one on November 11, 1978. If it's such an obvious question, then what's wrong with asking it?

"From the very outset, I answered the question 'Why?' categorically as being inappropriate at that point," Pastor Beveridge recalls. "That was because the answers we could propose were, to me, not sufficient at the time to meet the hurts of those who were suffering."

"I don't think asking 'Why?' answers any questions," Donna Van Beers says. "It just raises more questions."

"There is no room for the faithless question 'Why?' " writes Isobel Fleece in *Not By Accident,* the story of her teenage son's death and its aftermath.

It seems clear that we should not ask "Why?" Or should we? "Lots of people told us, 'Don't ask "Why," ' " Barbara Hayhurst says. "I thought about that a lot and one day I realized that when Jesus was on the cross He asked, 'My God, my God, *why* hast thou forsaken me?' If Jesus could ask 'Why?' then I think He wants me to do the same. But finding the answers is hard." Don Hayhurst has often said, "There's a reason for the accident and time will give us the answers."

It would be so nice to have the answers. It is unlikely we will get them unless we ask questions, however. Even the question "Why?" So let's ask. And let's ask other questions. We may not find answers, but since the Lord has not told us *not* to ask and since He has given answers in many other areas, who knows what we might find?

What about all the coincidences surrounding the accident. We know why the Bible study that Saturday was shifted to Randy Miller's apartment. We know that Brian Hayhurst drove that night only because Craig Cussimanio went to Syracuse. We know that Bonnie Furman and Johnny Hartman, two regulars, did not attend that evening. We know that the youngsters passed up pizza for Friendly's. We know that Henry Van Der Werf and Timmy Biscaye declined invitations to ride in the van and that Eric Borloz got out of Betty Grieve's car and into the van. That much we know, plus a lot more about things we might label as coincidences. One thing we definitely won't know is why all of them dovetailed that night.

What significance can be made of the notes that Maria Van Beers jotted down at the Bible study, one that had *five* points to it? And what do we make of the last verse she wrote down that night? That was James 1:5: "If any of you lack wisdom, let him ask of God, who giveth to all men liberally, and upbraideth not, and it shall be given him." This verse talks about asking God for wisdom. No, it doesn't specifically tell us to ask Him "Why?" But it *does* tell us to ask.

"I am usually a good sleeper," Pastor Beveridge says. "However, at the time of the accident I was preaching a series about Satan. I experienced a great deal of restlessness while sleeping. Twice on Saturday nights early in that series I woke up in a profuse sweat. The sheets were soaked. I had a sense of intense pressure upon me. I considered it more than a coincidence that at the time of the accident I was preaching such a series. When I learned about the accident, I couldn't help but think that we were now entering into an intense battle with the forces of the enemy. I am not one who believes Satan is behind every negative event, but one point I had made was that the devil propagandizes our immortality—the idea that we'll live forever. I had to think this all through and resolve it in my mind. I now feel that there really *was* satanic involvement in the accident . . . perhaps an attempt to finally divide the congregation."

By now there should be enough evidence to know if Satan succeeded. Pastor Beveridge says, "The death of the five kids helped greatly to bring the whole congregation together. It seemed to revitalize us and give us an appreciation for the fact that our charismatic brethren suffer as much as our noncharismatic brethren. And it showed people how they could help in a situation like this. John Richardson, a church member who was a strongly doctrinal noncharismatic, said shortly after the accident that we as a church suddenly saw how much our differences pale in the face of tragic events and that there was much we should emphasize about the faith we hold in common. The overwhelming reality was that we got God in a greater portion than ever before.

"It was just a few weeks before the accident that we came back from the retreat where we resolved the question about the charismatics' controversy. We can get so hung up with our systems of theology that we can't see what might be valid in someone else's position. I felt we should all work together and draw strength from each other. So I led the congregation in that way and a lot of us gave up our personal preferences for the good of the whole. It seemed appropriate, especially in light of the statement adopted long before I came to the church and which has been on the front of the church bulletin ever since. It reads: 'It is our conviction that the people of God can agree on the basic truths from God's Word. They can therefore worship, love, and serve Christ in unity of Spirit.' When it was announced in Church that Sunday evening that the leadership had come to this conclusion, some people were quite upset.

"The accident brought our church a spiritual unity, if only for a time. Our church will, of course, never be the same. The accident did things that could possibly never have been accomplished otherwise. It allowed us to build a bridge between factions and it increased our outreach by firmly linking us together. Many people have been drawn to the church as a result of the deaths of the five kids. We are 'the church that had the accident.' One woman recently lost a child in an accident and came to us because she remembered reading about the accident. As an evangelical (filled with the Spirit, I trust) I have grown in my respect for the charismatics in our congregation because of their walk with God, their love for Him. They have been a stimulating influence."

"The attitude of the church led to its growth," Don Hayhurst says. "Many have said they've walked into the church for the first time and have *sensed* that, 'This is the place.' "

PBC has grown. Since November 1978, the Sunday morning attendance has risen from three hundred fifteen to more than six hundred, with seven hundred fifty regulars. Membership has climbed from two hundred fifty-nine to three hundred twenty-five. Giving has increased from $186,500 to $382,000, with a $140,000 world missions budget. Currently, two Sunday worship services are held to accommodate the burgeoning growth. But do all these numbers, all the renewed lives, and the new church unity answer the "Why?" question?

Bruce Larson writes in *The Edge of Adventure:*

> I know a family, long considered the very "pillars of the church," in which mother, father, and all the children were active in church organizations, giving sacrificially of time, money, and leadership. One day the daughter was killed in an automobile accident while returning from a church conference. As far as I know, that family has not been inside the church since. This tragic accident reveals the motivation behind so much religious life and church service. These people served God at great cost to themselves, hoping to put Him in their debt and to buy some kind of insurance against the misfortunes of life. When God did not "keep His part of the bargain," they stopped serving Him.

Such words *cannot* be written about the four families, whose Christian strength and resiliency did much to encourage others at PBC and to attract others to the church. Much has been written about the grief and difficulties encountered by these families. Imagine the impact if all four families had reacted as did the one mentioned by Larson. If *one* family had turned against God, it surely would have aroused doubts in the minds of many about whether to put their trust in Him. Had *all* walked away from the Lord, it is hard to speculate about what might have happened. It would have been a cruel testimony that surely would have reverberated throughout the Pascack Valley.

As far as I know, no one has ever brought up this topic and the families themselves have never hinted that they feel they have had a tremendous effect for the cause of Christ. Let us not, however, underestimate how much the consistency of their faith has meant. And let us not think that their firmness has come easily. Everyone in the area knew about the accident and it thrust the families into prominence and virtually put them on public display. Many have watched them closely. They knew about the surgery that Howard Borloz and Larry Carroll had. The strength of the four families has been a blessing to perhaps more people than any of us will ever know.

Walt Van Beers points out that, "Many people wrote to us and said, 'We're looking at our children through new eyes. Now we know that life *can* be very, very short.' And people in the church stopped fooling around with their faith."

"We don't know who it was, but at the viewing someone whispered in Walter's ear and in my ear, 'You now have a new ministry,' " Connie Van Beers says. That ministry has been to counsel others who are grieving. From newspapers, the Van Beerses learn about who has died, and they often follow up by contacting the survivors. They write letters, send books they feel will be of help—*Not By Accident, A Child of God,* and *Good Grief*—have the people over for meals or visit their houses. Walt also became involved with putting on a series of films by Francis and Edith Schaeffer against abortion. This required months of training, preparation, setting up advertising and promotion, and then bringing the campaign to a conclusion. Walt, whom Dr. Beveridge correctly describes as being "extremely issue-conscious," now hopes to become involved with one of the groups trying to bring national attention to the shocking number of accidents and deaths caused by those who drive while under the influence of alcohol. "I think I might like to get involved with MADD [Mothers Against Drunk Drivers]," Walt says.

MADD, which was begun in 1980, and Remove Intoxicated Drivers, which started in 1978, have already demonstrated that there is a chance to win the war against drunk motorists. Largely because of their efforts, there has been a quick nationwide awakening to the unconscionable tolerance that lawmakers, the police, and society in general have shown toward drunk drivers. Doris Aiken, the founder of RID, points out that in 1980 "each drunk driver in New York paid, on the average, a twelve dollar fine, while those who killed a deer out of season had to pay $1,500."

Time reported in August 1981 that, "Someone is killed in a drunk-driving accident in the U.S. every 23 minutes, an annual average toll of more than 26,000." That's 52,000 in two years—more than the total number of Americans killed in battle during the Korean War (33,629) or in Vietnam (47,192), and it is almost as many as were lost during World War I (53,513). Another way to look at it is that, at the prevailing rate, it would take only six years to wipe out the equivalent of Little Rock, Arkansas (pop. 156,000), seven years to do away with Knoxville, Tennessee (182,000), and ten to dispose of Evansville, Indiana (134,000) *and* Columbia, South Carolina (115,000).

When we go back to trying to settle the whys surrounding November 11th, though, we have a Gordian knot—or at least one we can't untie with full assurance. Occasionally, the parents have wondered aloud about the whys. They have said things such as, "We know that because of the accident quite a few people have come to know the Lord and that others have been strengthened in their faith. But is that enough to justify the accident and all the pain?"

One person who was strengthened was Walter Bargman, who, together with his brother, Harry, runs Strunck's Delicatessen in Westwood.

"I got a call the morning after the accident and a voice said, 'Five kids from the church have died in an accident,' " Walter says. "I thought the person was talking about the church we had belonged to before we went to PBC. I knew that kids from there had gone on a retreat and I thought *they* were the ones in the accident. I knew *they* didn't know the Lord, and my heart sank. 'They're lost,' I thought. Then the voice gave me the names of the kids and I realized those youngsters weren't lost and that they'd gone to be with Jesus. That was it: The heart sinking when I thought of five young people going to eternity without Christ; my heart rejoicing when I realized it was actually five who were already in heaven with the Lord. That stressed to me the importance of eternity."

Walter had been a witness in various ways, but a week or two after the accident he began writing Bible verses on the chalkboard in the window where the daily specialties were advertised. Inside, in neat printing in chalk, right beside the day's menu, a new Bible verse also appears each day. One day it read:

HOT DOGS	With Jesus' help we will
HAMBURGERS	continually offer our sacrifice
ROAST TURKEY	of praise to God by telling others
HAM CAKES	of the glory of his name.
SPAGHETTI	Hebrews 13: vs 15
CORNED BEEF	
SOUPS	
CHICKEN NOODLE	JESUS LOVES YOU
MINESTRONE	JESUS IS KING OF KINGS
PEA	AND LORD OF LORDS
CREAM OF VEGETABLE	Praise God!

"It was as if the Lord showed me the need to be a witness for Him," Walter points out. "I see more boldness emerging because I see how important it is for people to hear. I used to be shy about it, but with Jesus behind me I knew I had to do it."

Couldn't the Lord have stirred Walter by using just one life? Why five? Why, too, did David arm himself with *five* smooth stones when all he needed to get the job done was one? Why five *smooth* stones? Why five smooth *stones?* Who knows? What the Bible tells us is that God accomplishes His purposes in hundreds of unique ways, many of which we humans would never have conceived of.

David was an unlikely one to challenge Goliath, but God accomplished His purpose through Him. God also used Emma Bunn in 1866. She had been one of the most troublesome youngsters at George Müller's huge orphanage in Bristol, England. Emma died not long after accepting Christ, but news of her stunning and complete turnaround had already spread. Her cantankerous ways had made Emma almost a legendary figure among her peers, and she had even more effect on them after she died. Right after her death came the *"most extensive and God-glorifying work ever wrought up to that time among the orphans.* In one house alone, three hundred and fifty were led to seek peace in believing." And it was all touched off by Emma.

Our society instills in us the belief that death is *the* end that is to be dreaded. God tells us this is not true. He never has promised that while on earth we would have a rose garden, but He has promised that our greatest blessings will come *after we die.* Heaven, God tells us, will be heavenly. In the words of Paul, that is the beginning of "life that is truly life."

In Psalms 116:15 we are told that, "Precious in the sight of the Lord is the death of his saints." In other words, He is happy to have those who have loved His Son come into His presence. Should Christians not share a similar joy?

God has *commanded* us to not put *anything* or *anyone* ahead of Him. We wrap so much of our lives around our loved ones that there is a danger of worshipping them more than God. That is a harsh indictment. But we must ask ourselves if we are complying with God's command. If we are, we should be able to see more of heaven and less of earth.

Think of death. How do you think you'll react when a loved one dies? Are you afraid of death? When you start looking at death, you will find some things that may well surprise you. You might find that death is, indeed, precious, and that it leads to a sort of Next

Supper. Look at death. Not just for a few minutes, but for periods of time. You really should look at death because it is the gateway to eternity for *you.*

The End

CHRISTIAN HERALD ASSOCIATION AND ITS MINISTRIES

CHRISTIAN HERALD ASSOCIATION, founded in 1878, publishes The Christian Herald Magazine, one of the leading interdenominational religious monthlies in America. Through its wide circulation, it brings inspiring articles and the latest news of religious developments to many families. From the magazine's pages came the initiative for CHRISTIAN HERALD CHILDREN'S HOME and THE BOWERY MISSION, two individually supported not-for-profit corporations.

CHRISTIAN HERALD CHILDREN'S HOME, established in 1894, is the name for a unique and dynamic ministry to disadvantaged children, offering hope and opportunities which would not otherwise be available for reasons of poverty and neglect. The goal is to develop each child's potential and to demonstrate Christian compassion and understanding to children in need.

Mont Lawn is a permanent camp located in Bushkill, Pennsylvania. It is the focal point of a ministry which provides a healthful "vacation with a purpose" to children who without it would be confined to the streets of the city. Up to 1000 children between the ages of 7 and 11 come to Mont Lawn each year.

Christian Herald Children's Home maintains year-round contact with children by means of an *In-City Youth Ministry*. Central to its philosophy is the belief that only through sustained relationships and demonstrated concern can individual lives be truly enriched. Special emphasis is on individual guidance, spiritual and family counseling and tutoring. This follow-up ministry to inner-city children culminates for many in financial assistance toward higher education and career counseling.

THE BOWERY MISSION, located at 227 Bowery, New York City, has since 1879 been reaching out to the lost men on the Bowery, offering them what could be their last chance to rebuild their lives. Every man is fed, clothed and ministered to. Countless numbers have entered the 90-day residential rehabilitation program at the Bowery Mission. A concentrated ministry of counseling, medical care, nutrition therapy, Bible study and Gospel services awakens a man to spiritual renewal within himself.

These ministries are supported solely by the voluntary contributions of individuals and by legacies and bequests. Contributions are tax deductible. Checks should be made out either to CHRISTIAN HERALD CHILDREN'S HOME or to THE BOWERY MISSION.

Administrative Office: 40 Overlook Drive, Chappaqua, New York 10514
Telephone: (914) 769-9000